AF837321

70 years of Population Policy

History of the Human Reproduction Program of the World Health Organisation 1950-2020

By

Louis-Marie Bonneau

with Grégor Puppinck

70 years of Population Policy: History of the Human Reproduction Program of the World Health Organisation 1950-2020

By Louis-Marie Bonneau with Grégor Puppinck

This book first published 2024

Ethics International Press Ltd, UK

British Library Cataloguing in Publication Data

A catalogue record for this book is available from the British Library

Copyright © 2024 by Louis-Marie Bonneau

All rights for this book reserved. No part of this book may be reproduced, stored in a retrieval system, or transmitted, in any form or by any means, electronic, mechanical photocopying, recording or otherwise, without the prior permission of the copyright owner.

Print Book ISBN: 978-1-80441-383-8

eBook ISBN: 978-1-80441-384-5

Table of Contents

Glossary

World Health Organization and its bodies:

WHO - World Health Organization: Created in 1948, its goal is to achieve the highest possible level of health for its member states. It defines health in its Constitution as "a state of complete physical, mental and social well-being and not merely the absence of disease or infirmity."

World Health Assembly (Health Assembly): Meeting annually in Geneva, Switzerland, the Assembly is WHO's highest decision-making body. It determines the policies of the Organization, appoints the Director-General, oversees financial policies, and approves the proposed budget for the Organization's programs.

Executive Board: Composed of 34 members elected for three years based on their technical qualifications, the WHO Executive Board sets the agenda of the World Health Assembly and the resolutions to be considered. It then ensures the implementation of the resolutions and policies decided by the Assembly.

Regional Committee: WHO Member States are divided into 6 regions (Africa, Europe, the Americas, the Eastern Mediterranean, South-East Asia, and the Western Pacific), each with a regional committee headed by a regional director.

ERC - *Ethics Review Committee*: an ethics review committee, composed of 27 members appointed by the Director-General, it reviews all research projects involving human beings and supported financially or technically by WHO.

SRH and HRP:

HRP - ***Human Reproduction Programme (UNDP/UNFPA/UNICEF/ WHO/World Bank Special Programme of Research, Development and Research Training in Human Reproduction):*** As a cosponsored programme, it has existed in this form since 1988. It is the main instrument of the United Nations system for research on human reproduction. During its 50 years of existence, it has changed its name several times.

RHR - ***Department of Reproductive Health and Research*:** former WHO department that became the SRH in 2019 and to which the HRP was attached since its creation in 1998.

SRH - ***Department of Sexual and Reproductive Health and Research*:** Department of Sexual and Reproductive Health and Research of WHO, to which the HRP belongs. SRH is in the UHC/Life Course division of WHO since the reorganization of the latter in 2019, when it replaces the HRP.

PCC - ***Policy and Coordination Committee*:** The *Policy and Coordination Committee* is responsible for coordinating the interests and activities of the cooperating parties of the Special Programme. It ensures the preparation and implementation of the Programme by reviewing reports and recommendations from the standing committee, the WHO implementing agency, and the *Scientific and Technical Advisory Group* (STAG), whose membership it approves. These reports and recommendations cover, among other things, the plan of action, budget, funding, and status updates on the Programme's progress toward its goals. It replaced the *Policy and Coordination Advisory Committee* (PCAC), which served a similar function from 1986 to 1988, during the establishment of the HRP co-sponsorship.

Standing committee: Standing Committee whose members are representatives of the Cosponsoring agencies of the Special Programme who meet three times a year to review the status of the Special

Programme and make recommendations to the *Policy and Coordination Committee* (PCC).

STAG - *Scientific and Technical Advisory Group*: Since 1986, its mission has been to review the scientific and technical content, size and scope of the Special Programme, including the research areas and approaches to be adopted. It also reviews the action plans and budget provided by WHO and makes recommendations on the priorities of the Special Programme or on the need to discontinue the activity of a *Task Force.*

RP2 - *Research Project Review Panel*: The Panel for the review of research projects, responsible for ensuring compliance with scientific practices and the quality of HRP research in terms of ethics, technique and financial aspects. Since 1988, it has replaced the *Review Group* which existed since the beginning of the Programme.

GAP - *Gender and Rights Advisory Panel*: Advisory Panel created in 1996 under the name of *Gender Advisory Panel* to focus on issues related to gender inequality, sexual mutilation and violence, and rights related to sexual practice and orientation. In 2007, it became the *Gender and Rights Advisory Panel* without changing its acronym.

Task forces: Working groups, which by virtue of their focused work, aim to accelerate the development and critical evaluation of new agents affecting fertility. These groups are working on the general understanding of human reproduction as well as on the study of products and processes that can be used for contraception and abortion.

Steering Committee: Steering Committee to develop the strategies to be implemented in each *Task Force.*

Research and Training Centres: WHO Research and Training Centers aimed at generating momentum in human reproductive research and promoting research collaboration, supporting training, organizing scientific conferences, and serving as regional documentation centers.

Clinical Research Centres: Clinical research centers designed to facilitate the rapid clinical evaluation of new fertility regulators.

PDRH - ***Programme Development in Reproductive Health*:** in charge of translating the results of the HRP into operational policies and actions, first within the RHR since 1998 and then within the SRH since 2019. The PDRH also works under the supervision of STAG.

RHT - ***Technical Support for Reproductive Health*:** Technical Support for Reproductive Health, a former WHO department, merged with HRP in 1998.

HRP co-sponsors:

UNFPA - ***United Nations Fund for Population Activities*:** Created in 1969, it is the lead UN agency for sexual and reproductive health issues.

UNICEF - ***United Nations International Children's Emergency Fund*:** A United Nations agency, created in 1946, with headquarters in New York, USA. It is responsible for protecting the rights of children worldwide, meeting their basic needs and promoting their full development.

World Bank: International financial institution, created in 1945, designed to support investments in developing countries. It has two goals: to end extreme poverty and to promote shared prosperity in a sustainable manner.

PNUD - ***United Nations Development Programme:*** Programme created in 1966, in charge of reducing poverty and inequality and promoting human development in a comprehensive way.

United Nations bodies and actions:

United Nations General Assembly: The deliberative, decision-making and representative body of the United Nations. Each of the 193 member states is represented.

Economic and Social Council (ECOSOC): A body responsible for coordination, dialogue and recommendations on economic, social and environmental issues, as well as the implementation of internationally agreed development goals. The Council oversees the work of specialized agencies in the economic, social and environmental fields. It is composed of 54 members elected for three-year terms and renewed by thirds.

World Population Conference: A series of five conferences, the last of which was held in 1994 in Cairo. These conferences adopted a Programme of Action calling for women's rights and reproductive health to be made a central issue in national and international economic and political development efforts, for access by all to comprehensive reproductive health care, including voluntary family planning, safe pregnancy and childbirth services, and for the prevention and treatment of sexually transmitted infections. It also argues that reproductive health and women's empowerment are interdependent and necessary for social progress.

Preface

By Giuseppe Benagiano, HRP director from 1993 to 1997.

I consider it a privilege to have been chosen to present Louis-Marie Bonneau's work on the population policy of the World Health Organization (WHO) and the developments that took place in the second half of the twentieth century and the first decades of the twenty-first. This is because of my work with the Organization for over fifty years.

This is an important study, as it carefully reconstructs the evolution of the United Nations (UN) system's involvement in the field of human reproduction and its many ramifications. Above all, this thesis shows how, from the second half of the twentieth century onwards, the World Health Organization (WHO) - the agency that for seventy-five years has overseen global health - has evolved by changing the direction and priorities of its involvement in the field of human reproduction.

WHO has been involved in issues concerning human reproduction since the 1950s, but initially the climate among member states was very conservative; for example, when, in 1951 the Indian Government requested WHO's help in introducing the so-called 'rhythm' method of Natural Family Planning, the reaction of some member states was rather negative. When, in 1954, it was suggested that WHO should take part in the first UN World Population Conference in Rome, devoted to an exchange of scientific information on demographic variables, their determinants and consequences, some member states were so opposed that they threatened to leave the Organization.

In other words, at the time, it was almost inconceivable to link health to the demographic explosion. In this climate, it took more than 10 years before Dr. Marcolino Gomes Candau, then Director-General of the WHO, was able to state publicly that human reproductive problems represented a major public health issue.

However, once the ice was broken, as shown in detail in this book, progress was steady and rapid: in 1965, WHO created a *Human Reproduction Unit* with a mandate that included advising member states on family planning. This was a complete change from the attitudes of just 10 years ago. The Unit gradually evolved into the 'Expanded' (and later 'Special') Programme for Research, Development and Training in Human Reproduction (Human Reproduction Programme, HRP), officially created in 1972 with funding from a few northern European countries and the Ford Foundation, as this thesis outlines.

Initially, the Programme aimed to develop a variety of safe, acceptable and effective family planning methods for fertility regulation. This objective was achieved through task-oriented Working Groups. The HRP was also responsible for monitoring the long-term safety and efficacy of existing methods. This thesis details this research work from 1972 to the present day. It highlights the various techniques developed and tested: intrauterine devices, implantable hormonal devices, injectable contraceptives, sterilization, immunocontraception, the introduction of medical abortion, male hormonal contraceptives and behavioral studies on the acceptability of the techniques used.

Finally, the Programme was to create and support Institutions capable of working with WHO in the field of human reproduction; this was achieved through a network of Collaborating Centres in the six WHO Regions and the creation of four Research and Training Centres. This infrastructure has enabled the HRP to play a leading role in generating evidence of efficacy and safety, and in translating research data into action. It should be emphasized that, from the outset, the focus was on fertility regulation, but work was also carried out on infertility.

An important development took place in 1988, when the United Nations Development Programme (UNDP), the United Nations Population Fund (UNFPA) and the World Bank joined WHO as official co-sponsors of the HRP. More recently, the United Nations Children's Fund (UNICEF) has also joined the Programme. This partnership has increased both the visibility and funding of the HRP. This thesis also notes that a non-governmental organization, the International Planned Parenthood Federation (IPPF), has been a permanent member of the program's Coordinating Committee since 1977, alongside the program's co-sponsors.

Another major development took place at the World Conference on Population and Development (ICPD) held in Cairo in 1994. For this occasion, HRP was tasked with defining a new socio-medical entity: Reproductive Health, which was subsequently transformed into Sexual and Reproductive Health and Rights. The HRP was then charged with informing the world's women and men of the existence of multiple human rights that protect them, including the right to life and health, the right to privacy, the right to reproductive and sexual education, and the prohibition of discrimination. A further development took place in 1998, when the HRP merged with WHO's Division of Reproductive Health Technical Support (RHT).

With great foresight, Dr. Alexander Kessler, the first head, and since then Director, of the HRP had declared that special programmes do not last forever: they are intended to solve "urgent but limited problems". In reality, the HRP has already survived half a century, celebrating fifty years of life in 2022. This has been made possible by a gradual evolution of its objectives and structures: it was for this reason that the new Department of Reproductive Health and Research (RHR) was set up to ensure a continuous dialogue between research and the process of knowledge exchange, advocacy and technical support for national programmes. The merger with RHT enabled HRP to further extend its work to the full range of reproductive health and sexual relations issues, including AIDS research. More recently, a new name has been established for the department, that of Sexual and Reproductive Health and Research (SRH).

Notably, the new department has moved into the field of pregnancy termination, developing an effective regimen for non-surgical abortion and demonstrating that primary care providers can safely administer such a regimen, as well as undertaking manual vacuum aspiration for first-trimester abortions.

After the start of the new millennium, thanks to its advocacy activities, the HRP, in 2004, made a major contribution to the development and adoption of the Global Reproductive Health Strategy by the World Health Assembly. The RHR/HRP Department also played a role in the formulation of the 2004 revision of the ICPD goals and in the definition of the Millennium Development Goals for "reproductive health for all by 2015" in 2006.

The Special Programme therefore evolved gradually in the 2000s, just as Dr. Kessler had predicted. The new department now deals with sexually transmitted infections (including HIV/AIDS), family planning, infertility, unsafe abortion, sexual health, cervical cancer screening in developing countries, and sexual and reproductive rights.

New activities also include promoting international cooperation in the field of human reproduction, promoting inter-agency statements on the implications for public health, women's rights against female genital mutilation, and sex-specific selection. An important new activity has been the creation of guidelines and tools, such as the "Medical Eligibility Criteria for Contraceptive Use," the "Global Handbook for Family Planning Agents," the "Definition of Core Competencies in Primary Health Care," and the design of tools to operationalize a humane and women's rights-based approach to sexual and reproductive health programmes.

In conclusion, today, HRP/SRH supports and coordinates research on a global scale, synthesizes research findings through systematic literature reviews, builds research capacity in low-income countries and develops dissemination tools on how to effectively use the information that research is constantly uncovering.

All these developments and innovations are detailed in the book.

Introduction

Until now, the literature on the *Human Reproduction Programme* (HRP) had been written by former members of the Programme, in particular former directors. Other articles existed but took a macro-analytical approach. The aim of this research was to take an outside look at the HRP, taking a more micro-analytical approach and contextualizing it as exhaustively as possible. The goal was to provide research with a synthesis based almost exclusively on primary sources, in order to gain the most accurate understanding of the institutional path leading to research on human reproduction at the WHO. These sources are mainly WHO and UN resolutions, WHO Director-General reports, and HRP reports. The aim was also to understand how this WHO programme and strategy for human reproduction fit into the broader UN vision. The goal was also to determine how influences and orientations, both in terms of research and societal vision, were organized and concretized within the HRP's actions. Finally, this research aimed to determine the impact of the HRP on contemporary scientific policies and recommendations concerning human reproduction. Indeed, understanding the genealogy of these policies and recommendations will enable us to better apprehend and question them today.

The UN's and WHO's analyses and strategies on population and human reproduction took decades to develop. It also took several years for their vision to be realized in the HRP as we know it today, which has undergone several structural and strategic evolutions over the course of its existence. As early as the 1950s, the UN was expressing concern about "demographic problems." This concern was primarily economic, as population growth was seen as impoverishing the population. As a specialized agency of the UN and considering that it was also degrading the population's state of health, the WHO therefore took an interest in this phenomenon. To meet this new challenge, it was decided in 1964 to increase scientific research of human reproduction. Thus, from an economic concern and a health concern, WHO defined its strategy in resolution WHA18.49 and created the *Human Reproduction Unit* in 1965. WHO's aim was to regulate the population in order to improve the health situation. This vision was approved by the UN in 1966. The WHO took on four roles: an advisory role in the promotion of family planning, a coordinating role, a documentary and biomedical research role, and a training role.

In 1970, several organizations met in Geneva to discuss the creation of a worldwide research programme on human reproduction within the framework of the *Human Reproduction Unit*. Following a feasibility study strongly supported by the Ford Foundation, a draft programme was drawn up in 1971. The programme was then built around an action plan that saw the creation of at least four major *Research and Training Centres*. The plan also envisaged a model of cooperation with clinical centers to "facilitate the rapid clinical evaluation of new fertility regulating agents." The creation of *Task Forces* was then an important component of the imagined Programme. Their role was to conduct research projects and increase collaboration in research and development in the field of fertility regulation. The aim was to provide a flexible mechanism through the formation of groups which, through their focused work, would aim to "accelerate the development and critical evaluation of new agents affecting fertility." Thus, as early as 1971, the *new Expanded Programme for Research, Development and Training in Human Reproduction* (HRP) was directed by an *Advisory Group* charged with advising WHO on research policy, strategies and priorities, as well as resource allocation.

The Programme was conceived from a demographic angle, but from a practical point of view, it became part of the WHO's role as coordinator of biomedical research with resolution WHA25.60 of 1972. According to various Programme Directors, this 1972 resolution formally established the HRP. Between 1970 and 1973, contributors to the Programme included Sweden, Canada, Denmark, and the Ford Foundation.

In 1977, the Expanded Programme became the Special Programme, and in 1986 a transformation of its structure began. The *Advisory Group* became the *Policy and Coordination Advisory Committee* (PCAC). This committee comprised the twelve main contributing countries; twelve members were elected by the regional committees, three members elected by the PCAC (who could represent NGOs), as well as UNFPA, the World Bank and IPPF as permanent members. The programme also added the *Scientific and Technical Advisory Group* (STAG) to its supervisory bodies.

In 1987, UNDP, UNFPA, WHO and the World Bank decided to co-sponsor the Programme in order to secure substantial, stable funding. Since 1988, this new form of the Programme has remained essentially the same. The PCAC became the PCC (*Policy and Coordination Committee*) and the new structure was administered by a *Standing Committee,* whose members are representatives of the co-sponsoring institutions. The Health Assembly approved the new structure in resolution WHA41.9. In 1996, the *Gender Advisory Panel* (GAP) was also set up, to give particular attention to issues relating to gender inequality, genital mutilation, sexual violence, and rights linked to sexual practice and orientation.

In 1998, HRP merged with the *Division of Technical Support for Reproductive Health* (RHT) to form the *Department of Reproductive Health and Research* (RHR). RHR comprised HRP on the one hand, and the *Programme Development in Reproductive Health* (PDRH) on the other. The HRP remained a research and training programme with no operational activities. The PDRH's mission thus became the implementation of the HRP's results into operational policies and actions within the RHR. In December 2012, UNICEF became a new co-sponsor of the HRP and UNAIDS became a new permanent member of the PCC, joining IPPF in this capacity. Finally, as part of a wider WHO reform, the RHR was placed under the responsibility of the WHO Division of *UHC/Life Course* and became the *Department of Sexual and Reproductive Health and Research* (SRH) in 2019.

Scientific orientation of the programme

The programme's activities have enabled it to be at the forefront of research into human reproduction and family planning, notably through the collaboration of *Task Forces, Clinical Research Centres, and Research* and *Training Centres*. Research has focused on the safety and efficacy of fertility regulation methods, the behavioral and social determinants of fertility regulation, fertility regulation vaccines, male fertility regulation methods, natural fertility regulation methods, and infertility prevention and management.

All aspects of human reproduction were studied to determine how new contraceptives and abortifacients could be developed. It was soon established that male contraception was the most difficult to implement. Without completely abandoning this aspect, the programme concentrated on female contraception. This involved, for example, interfering with the transport of the ovum by non-surgical chemical means, creating anti-pregnancy or anti-sperm vaccines, developing new generations of contraceptive pills with fewer side-effects, or implanting intra-uterine devices (IUDs). To give an example of whose influence is clearly visible today, one line of research was the development of "emergency contraception," i.e., the "morning-after pill." Other research focused on prostaglandins, with the aim of developing safe and effective methods of second-trimester abortion. Still, other research integrated sociological and psychological aspects, notably on the after-effects of abortions or on their acceptability, as well as on the acceptability of contraception and sterilization.

The HRP's research network also enabled it to conduct large-scale clinical trials for its work. At the same time, the HRP disseminated guides and guidelines on family planning, including female sterilization and natural methods. Today, it is clear that the HRP's role was fundamental in the development of the most commonly used methods of contraception and abortion. In the space of 50 years, a subject which was almost taboo in many countries, and for which methods were still very limited, has become a field of research in its own right; and birth control with the declared aim of limiting the number of births has become an acceptable and even highlighted subject.

According to a 2013 evaluation report,[1] HRP is seen as the "unique global resource that generates the research findings, synthesizes the evidence and develops the products to support policy formulation and programme strengthening to improve SRH."[2] The Programme also benefits from the image of the WHO, which, according to the report, is perceived worldwide as "inclusive and neutral," as well as a universally recognized authority in its field. This image ensures the HRP's credibility with member states and increases the impact of the documents it publishes.[3] According to a report from another 2019[4] evaluation, "as a programme cosponsored by four UN agencies and the World Bank, HRP fills a unique and critical role as a global authority for evidence on issues of human reproduction, sexual health, and sexual rights. HRP is embedded in WHO, which provides it with a close link to the authority that defines global norms and standards in the health sector and supports countries in their application. While the co-sponsorship and distinct funding model provides a greater degree of freedom from political influence in the pursuit of evidence. The work of HRP focuses on priority issues of sexual and reproductive health and rights in low- and middle-income countries. Among its scope of activities, HRP was particularly well placed to synthesize and build consensus around existing evidence, including global data and indicators. This is an area of work in which HRP has an undisputed leadership role. As a research agency, HRP maintains an essential role

[1] World Health Organization [WHO], *External Evaluation 2008-2012: Advancing Sexual and Reproductive Health: Executive Summary*, (2013), https://apps.who.int/iris/handle/10665/85332 [hereinafter *External Evaluation 2008-2012*].

[2] *Id.* at 9.

[3] *Id.* at 8-9.

[4] World Health Organization [WHO], *External Evaluation of the UNDP-UNFPA-UNICEF-WHO-World Bank Special Programme of Research, Development and Research Training in Human Reproduction (HRP) 2013-2017*, (2019), https://cdn.who.int/media/docs/default-source/hrp/hrp-evaluation-report-vol-1.pdf?sfvrsn=140faddc_6&download=true [hereinafter *HRP 2013-2017*].

in niche areas such as the prevention of unsafe abortion and the promotion of sexual rights where there are few global players." [5]

The philosophical orientation of the programme

The Programme has originated in the demographic concerns of the United Nations in the 1950s, in the face of the increase in the earth's population. In a logical extension, G. Benagiano and E. Diczfalusy, two former HRP leaders, published an article in 1995 in which they placed the HRP in a filiation beginning with Condorcet, then Malthus and ending with Margaret Sanger:[6]

> It is therefore increasingly being realised today that the global ecosystem imposes limits on the number of people the world can sustain. A Chinese proverb says: "Do not think that you are on the wrong path, simply because you have not gone far enough". Malthus was not wrong… In retrospect, it is clear that Malthus was a brilliant thinker and philosopher. However, he is not the "father" of family planning; the idea of fertility regulation was simply unacceptable to his conventional Christian philosophy. The intellectual father of family planning was the Marquis de Condorcet. Bertrand Russell points out that Condorcet originated Malthus's theory of population, which, however, did not have for him the gloomy consequences that it had for Malthus, because he coupled it with the necessity of active birth control Malthus's father was a disciple of Condorcet, and it was in this way that Malthus came to know the theory. Interestingly, Condorcet, like the somewhat later Charles Fourier, was also a pioneer in advocating equality for women. William Faulkner says that "the past is never dead; it is not even past…". If Condorcet is the "father" of family planning with its demographic rationale, the "mother" must be Margaret Sanger. She opened her family

---

[5] *Id.* at VI.

[6] Giuseppe Benagiano & Egon Diczfalusy, *Research on Human Reproduction and the United Nations*, 85 S. AFR. MED. J. 370, 371-73 (1995).

> planning clinic in Brooklyn, New York, on October 16, 1916. It instantly became very popular until, after 11 days, the police department closed it down and Mrs. Sanger was sentenced by a New York court and imprisoned for "obscenity". Mrs. Sanger can therefore be considered the "mother" of practical family planning with its human rights and reproductive health rationale.

Today, the HRP's aim is to meet the contraceptive and family planning information needs of 225 to 270 million women living in developing countries. These needs are not being met because of "fear or experience of side-effects; limited access and choice; cultural or religious opposition; and poor quality of available services." Access to these services would then be "crucial for securing the well-being and autonomy of women, while supporting the health and development of communities."[7] So for the HRP, "Ensuring access to preferred contraceptive methods for women and couples is essential to securing their well-being and autonomy, while supporting the health and development of communities."[8] This project goes hand in hand with an idealistic vision, reflected in statements made by the Programme Director in 2004, for example, that "there is an urgent need now to recognize the key role of reproductive health in underpinning sustainable development, and to increase our efforts, not only to build the evidence base for effective action, but also to put into practice what we already know. Only in this way can we move towards our ideal world."[9] Or in 2008: "On the eve of my departure from WHO, I am reminded of the words of Benjamin Mays, "It isn't a disgrace not to reach the stars, but it is a disgrace to have no stars to reach for." Let us make sure the sexual and reproductive health and well-being of our

---

[7] World Health Organization [WHO], *HRP Annual Report 2016*, at 4 (2017), https://apps.who.int/iris/handle/10665/255768 [hereinafter *Annual Report 2016*].
[8] World Health Organization [WHO], *HRP Annual Report 2020*, at 8 (2021), https://apps.who.int/iris/handle/10665/346657 [hereinafter *HRP Annual Report 2020*].
[9] World Health Organization [WHO], *Research on Reproductive Health at WHO: Pushing the Frontiers of Knowledge: Biennial Report 2002-2003*, at 7-8 (2004), https://apps.who.int/iris/handle/10665/42997 [hereinafter *Biennial Report 2002-2003*].

fellow human beings, wherever they live, is one of the stars in our lives."[10]

These scientific and philosophical orientations have had a major impact on the world's population right up to the present day. Scientific research can have major societal implications and is therefore never neutral in itself. Such is the case with research into human reproduction. It would seem that the fear, fueled by scientific discourse, of a global crisis linked to a demographic explosion has conditioned the policies of many of the world's countries. This raises the question of the relationship between science and politics, particularly when the latter is confronted with its own fears, especially in times of crisis. This question is all the more pressing when, without disputing the robustness of the scientific results and method, it becomes apparent that the research agenda is influenced by a limited number of states and private players, who are the main funders and administrators of the Programme. Faced with the fear of a crisis linked to a demographic explosion, it was decided to focus scientific research on fertility control by developing contraceptive and family planning methods. Forty years later, it's time to assess and critique the results.

****

[10] World Health Organization [WHO], *Sexual and Reproductive Health: Research and Action in Support of the Millennium Development Goals, Biennial Report 2006-2007*, at 1-3 (2008), https://apps.who.int/iris/handle/10665/43916 [hereinafter *Biennial Report 2006-2007*].

Institutional context: WHO structure and link with the UN

WHO is a specialized agency of the United Nations whose Constitution was approved on July 22, 1946, at the end of the International Health Conference. WHO began its activity on April 7, 1948. Like all UN specialized agencies, the relationship is established individually, and the agency is legally independent. Within the UN, its action is coordinated with other agencies and services by the Economic and Social Council. This Council is the body responsible for coordination, dialogue, and recommendations on economic, social and environmental issues; as well as in the implementation of internationally agreed development goals. The Council oversees the work of the specialized agencies in the economic, social and environmental fields. The WHO and the UN share information, data and administrative and technical resources. Through their cooperation, they ensure the avoidance duplication of research and projects.

The governance of WHO is divided into three entities: the World Health Assembly, the Executive Board, and the Director-General. Meeting annually in Geneva, Switzerland, the Health Assembly is WHO's highest decision-making body. It determines the policies of the Organization, appoints the Director-General, oversees financial policies and approves the proposed budget for the Organization's programs. The WHO Executive Board, composed of 34 members elected for three-year terms and on the basis of their technical qualifications, sets the agenda for the World Health Assembly and the resolutions to be considered there. It then ensures the implementation of the resolutions and policies decided by the Health Assembly. Elected for a five-year term, renewable once, the Director-General directs the administration of the Organization.

WHO's budget is determined on the one hand by fixed contributions from member states and on the other hand by voluntary contributions from state and non-state actors. For the period 2021-2022, the United States is the largest contributor (US$ 1,122.7 million - 16% of funding), followed by the Bill and Melinda Gates Foundation (US$ 800.6 million - 12.7% of funding).

To achieve its mission, WHO forms a large number of partnerships and networks to support research coordination, provide financial support to countries in need, and create a common working space for different health actors, whether private investors, public administrations, NGOs, foundations or academic institutions. WHO also directly administers inter-agency programs (e.g. UNAIDS), secretariats for the follow-up of international conventions involving the Organization, and co-sponsored programmes (*Special Programme on Research and Training in Tropical Diseases* - TDR, *Special Programme of Research, Development and Research Training in Human Reproduction* - HRP, *Global Polio Eradication Initiative* - GPEI). In accordance with the resolutions of the various conferences on population, and expressing for the United Nations the concern of the States for the demographic question, the WHO leads with the HRP a joint Programme with the UNDP, the UNFP, the UNICEF, and the World Bank. This programme seeks to support research and to push the States and the scientific and medical communities in the fields of sexual and reproductive health. The Programme focuses much of its research on birth control, including the development of contraceptives and abortifacients. It also focuses research on the health and sociological consequences of their use.

PART ONE

"Population problems": a concern of the UN and WHO since the 1950s

Chapter 1
WHO's role in the United Nations system

"WHO is the directing and coordinating authority for health within the United Nations system."[11] Its Constitution[12] was adopted by the representatives of 61 States at the International Health Conference held in New York from June 19 to July 22, 1946. According to article 1 of the constitution, "the objective of the World Health Organization [...] shall be the attainment by all peoples of the highest possible level of health". To this end, WHO acts as a directing and coordinating authority in the field of health, establishes collaborations with other international, governmental or non-governmental organizations that it deems relevant, and has the role of stimulating and guiding research in the field of health (art. 2). Article 2.l. states that in order to achieve its purpose, the Organization shall seek "to promote maternal and child health and welfare and to foster the ability to live harmoniously in a changing total environment."

Structure and functioning of WHO

According to Article 9 of its Constitution, the functioning of the Organization is carried out by the World Health Assembly (Health Assembly), the Executive Board, and the Secretariat. The Health Assembly is composed of delegates representing the Member States (Article 10). Article 18 defines the functions of the Health Assembly. In particular, it is responsible for determining the policy of the Organization, appointing the Director-General, considering and approving the reports and activities of the Board and the Director-General; considering recommendations relating to health from the

---

[11] *World Health Organization*, UNITED NATIONS, https://www.un.org/youthenvoy/2013/09/who-world-health-organisation/ (last visited July 5, 2023).

[12] WHO, *Constitution of the World Health Organization*, *in* BASIC DOCUMENTS (49th ed., 2020), https://apps.who.int/gb/bd/pdf_files/BD_49th-en.pdf#page=6.

General Assembly of the United Nations and the Economic and Social Council; and encouraging or directing all research work in the field of health by using the staff of the Organization or establishing its own institutions.

The Director-General is appointed by the Health Assembly on the proposal of the Board under whose authority he is placed. He is the chief technical and administrative officer of the Organization (Article 31). He appoints the staff of the Secretariat in accordance with the Staff Rules (Article 35). In the performance of their duties, the Director-General and the staff shall not seek or receive instructions from any government or from any authority external to the Organization (Article 37). The technical and administrative staff of the Organization shall enjoy such privileges and immunities as are necessary for the free exercise of their functions in connection with the Organization (Article 67).

A focus on "population problems" from the beginning

As early as 1950, a resolution of the Third World Health Assembly[13] invited the WHO Director-General to collaborate on a broad basis with the United Nations and the specialized agencies in all matters relating to "population problems."[14]

In August 1951, the WHO Regional Committee for South-East Asia published a document entitled *"Population Problems."* The Director-General drew the Members of the executive board's attention to this

---

[13] World Health Organization [WHO], Res. WHA3.7, *On Population Problems,* (May 19, 1950), *in* 3d World Health Assembly Geneva, Part I: Resolutions and Decisions, at 17 (1950) ,
https://apps.who.int/iris/bitstream/handle/10665/86205/WHA3.7_eng.pdf?sequence=1&isAllowed=y.
[14] WHO, *Resolution on Population Problems*, 5th Sess. Geneva, pt. 1 at. 9 (1950), https://apps.who.int/iris/handle/10665/85604.

document in November of that year.[15] It reported that on the recommendation of the UN Commission on Population and Development, a survey was conducted in India on "Inter-relationship between economic, social and population changes."[16] One purpose of the survey was to determine the awareness of various demographic groups of artificial birth control methods.[17] This region of the world received particular attention at the time, since half of the total world population growth was taking place in Asia. The paper went on to note that while before the eighteenth century, the death rate had been the major factor governing population growth, medical and technological advances had caused it to fall. Nuptiality and fertility were then considered factors to be taken into account to govern the demographic growth.[18] For the WHO Regional Committee for South-East Asia, the issue of family limitation was of great interest in India, particularly in terms of convincing the population that limiting births would be of economic and social benefit. The Indian Sub-Committee on Population and Family Planning recommended to the *Indian Planning Commission* that the State provide the necessary means for sterilization, or to advise on the application of contraceptive methods. In the same vein, the Ministry of Health of the Government of India had also requested WHO assistance for a pilot family planning experiment (known as "rhythmic control").[19]

According to an article[20] published by Giuseppe Benagiano (director of the HRP from 1993 to 1997), the WHO became interested in human reproduction after this request for technical assistance from the Indian

---

[15] WHO, *SEA/RC4/14 – Population Problems*, Reg'l Comm. for S.E. Asia, New Delhi (Aug. 17, 1951), https://apps.who.int/iris/bitstream/handle/10665/128144/EB9_16_eng.pdf?sequence=1&isAllowed=y.

[16] *Id.* at 3.

[17] *Id.* at 4.

[18] *Id.* at 5.

[19] *Id.* at 11-12.

[20] Giuseppe Benagiano et al., *The Special Programme of Research in Human Reproduction : Forty Years of Activities to Achieve Reproductive Health for All*, 74 GYNECOLOGIC & OBSTETRIC INVESTIGATION 190, 191 (2012).

government on natural family planning (NFP) methods. In 1952, an Executive Council document on a "*Pilot study on the voluntary limitation of families in India*" was published.[21] He recalls that this request from the Indian government was subject to the condition that the experiments be "restricted to the use of the "safe period" only and without the use of mechanical contrivances." Dr. Abraham Stone, vice president of the *Planned Parenthood Association,* was hired by WHO to conduct this preliminary survey in India. These pilot family planning studies, conducted in collaboration with the *Division of Population Studies,* and with the assistance of two WHO field officers, were completed in 1954 and a report was submitted to the Indian government.[22] An article in the quarterly review of the *Institut national d'études démographique* of 1955 gives an account of it.[23]

In support of its argument, the 1951 document of the WHO Regional Committee for Southeast Asia[24] recommends to Southeast Asian governments interested in the issue of population control the findings of a 1948 report entitled "*Public Health and Demography in the Far East*" by Dr. M.C. Balfour and his colleagues at the Rockefeller Foundation. According to this report, "the level of fertility [...] is a product of the total culture, including its most deeply laid and intimate aspects which are slow to change. Profound changes in fertility will probably await profound changes in the culture and economy."[25] In general, Dr. M.C. Balfour advocated reducing fertility in marriage and he did not hesitate to propose the most radical methods: "There are some possibilities in

---

[21] WHO Executive Board, EB9/96, *Pilot Study on the Voluntary Limitation of Families in India,* (January 28, 1952), https://apps.who.int/iris/handle/10665/128229.
[22] WHO Reg'l Office S.E. Asia, SEA/RC7/2, *Population Studies,* at 55 (1954) https://apps.who.int/iris/handle/10665/130998.
[23] Q. Rev. Nat'l Inst. for Demographic Stud., *Survey on the Possibility of Disseminating the Ogino Method in India,* 10 POPULATION 361-65 (1955) https://www.persee.fr/doc/pop_0032-4663_1955_num_10_2_4364.
[24] WHO Reg'l Comm. for S.E. Asia, SEA/RC4/14, *Population Problems,* (1951), https://apps.who.int/iris/bitstream/handle/10665/128144/EB9_16_eng.pdf?sequence=1&isAllowed=y.
[25] *Id.* at 6.

sterilization where medical facilities are available. We think, however, that main reliance must be placed on contraception."[26]

Finally, also in this 1951 document, the WHO Regional Committee for South-East Asia, referring to resolution WHA3.7 of 1950, also states the position of the Executive Board, which emphasized the need for WHO to take concrete action on population problems and to provide advice on the medical problems posed by population limitation.[27] This position led to a resolution adopted by the same Council which, noting the collaboration established between the World Health Organization and the United Nations on population problems, invited the Director-General to study these problems in conjunction with the United Nations Population Commission, with a goal to define the functions of the two organizations.[28]

---

[26] *Id.* at 8.

[27] *Id.* at 9-10.

[28] *Id.* at 10.

Chapter 2
Economic problems or better global health: the beginnings of human reproduction research (1954-1966)

Between economic and demographic problems: a concern of the UN

In 1954, the first World Population Conference was held in Rome.[29] The aim of this conference was to gather scientific information on demographic variables, their determinants, and their consequences.[30] Different meetings dealt with different demographic aspects of economic and social development: "Population in relation to the development of non-biological resource; Population in relation to the development of agriculture; Population in relation to capital formation, investment and employment; Demographic aspects of economic and social development." [31] In the opinion of Egon Diczfalusy (a collaborator with Alexander Kessler, the first director of the HRP, and a senior consultant to the HRP from 1984 to 1996) in a 1985 article[32], the immediate impact of this conference was little or nonexistent on policy makers.

---

[29] World Population Conf., *Proceedings of the World Population Conference*, U.N. Doc. E/CONF 13/412, meetings 20, 22, 24, and 26 (1955), https://documents-dds-ny.un.org/doc/UNDOC/GEN/NL5/502/64/PDF/NL550264.pdf?OpenElement.

[30] Conferences | Population, UN, https://www.un.org/fr/conferences/population/index (last visited July 5, 2023).

[31] E/CONF 13/412, Preface

[32] E. Diczfalusy, *World Health Organization Special Programme of Research, Development and Research Training in Human Reproduction. An international response to a global concern*, Contraception 323, 324 (Oct. 1985) https://www.sciencedirect.com/science/article/abs/pii/0010782485900368.

The statement of a close relationship between economic and demographic problems

In 1957, the United Nations General Assembly resolution 1217 (XII)[33] considered "that there is a close relationship between economic problems and population problems," Considering the resolutions of the General Assembly and the Economic and Social Council on the relationship between economic and social development, the resolution invited "States Members, particularly those which are in the process of economic development, to follow as closely as possible the interrelationships existing between economic and population change." In 1962, resolution 1838 (XVII)[34] went on to refer to demography as a "problem" especially in "less developed" countries. It thus requested that a factual inventory be conducted on this relationship between demography and economic development. The Secretary General was asked to conduct a survey on this issue, particularly in the member states.

A willingness to research to better respond to the demographic challenge

Resolution 1048 (XXXVII)[35] of 1964 of the Economic and Social Council of the United Nations, reported on this investigation entrusted to the Secretary General. It reported "the serious concern expressed in reply to the inquiry by many governments of developing countries, about the slow rate of economic growth of their countries in relation to the high rate of their population growth." The Economic and Social Council of

---

[33] United Nations: G.A. Res. 1217 (XII) (Dec. 14, 1957), https://documents-dds-ny.un.org/doc/RESOLUTION/GEN/NR0/120/00/PDF/NR012000.pdf?OpenElement.

[34] United Nations: G.A. Res. 1838 (XVII) (Dec. 8, 1962), https://digitallibrary.un.org/record/204294?ln=en (referring to G.A. Res. 1217 (XII) of 1957).

[35] United Nations: Economic and Social Council Res. 1048 (XXXVII), *On Population Growth and Economic and Social Development, August 1964*, A/18/P&B/4, Annex A (Apr. 27, 1965), https://apps.who.int/iris/handle/10665/136768?search-result=true&query=%22WHA18_PB-4%22&scope=%2F&rpp=10&sort_by=score&order=desc (referring to resolution 1838 (XVII) of 1962).

the United Nations then invited the General Assembly to take these results into account and requested the Secretary-General to communicate them to the WHO so that it consider the results in its program. Finally, the resolution "urges the Secretary-General and the specialized agencies concerned to explore ways and means of strengthening and expanding their work in the field of population, including the possibilities of obtaining voluntary contributions."

Similarly, a 1965 resolution[36] outlined the organization's work program and priorities in the population fields. In particular, it called for the improvement of population statistics and the strengthening of regional population research and training centers, following the recommendations of the Population Commission[37] in the report of its thirteenth session. It then requested that the Secretary General provide[38] "advisory services and training on action programmes in the field of population at the request of Governments desiring assistance in this field" while coordinating these activities with specialized institutions interested in population-related issues.

Finally, the Second World Population Conference was held in Belgrade in 1965.[39] During this conference, the emphasis was placed on the

---

[36] United Nations: Economic and Social Council Res. 1084 (XXXIX), *On Work Programmes and Priorities in Population Fields,* (July 1965), https://digitallibrary.un.org/record/214117?ln=en (referring to G.A. Res. 1838 (XVII) of 1962 and 1048 (XXXVII) of 1964).

[37] "The Commission on Population and Development (CPD) works with the United Nations (UN) system to monitor and review the implementation of the Programme of Action of the International Conference on Population and Development (ICPD). It is a functional commission of the United Nations Economic and Social Council (ECOSOC)." Commission de la Population et du Développement Fiche d'information [Commission of Population and Development Factsheet], p. 1, https://www.youthdoit.org/assets/Uploads/CPD-Factsheet-french-def.pdf.

[38] In accordance with Council Resolution 222 (IX) of August 1949 and General Assembly Resolution 418 (V) of December 1950.

[39] World Population Conf., *Proceedings of the World Population Conference, Volume III: Projections measurement of Population trends,* U.N. Doc. E/CONF.41/4, at B.8 pp. 267-308 (1965), https://documents-dds-ny.un.org/doc/UNDOC/GEN/N67/191/41/PDF/N6719141.pdf?OpenElement.

"analysis of fertility as part of development planning policy,"[40] thus also studying the relationship between demography and economic development.[41] This conference and these studies took place at a time when the U.S. Agency for International Development (USAID) was beginning to fund population programs.[42]

WHO's response to this new UN issue: fertility regulation for better global health

In the years that followed, the WHO devised a response to the UN's demographic concerns, through the prism of health. The aim was to motivate research in human reproduction and to make it effective. We will therefore show how the World Health Organization started from a worrying demographic observation to create a research body: the *Human Reproduction Unit*. We will then highlight the WHO's strategy of conducting research on fertility to regulate the population and thus improve the health situation. Finally, we will show how the UN approved this vision and strategy.

---

[40] CONFERENCES | POPULATION, UN, https://www.un.org/en/conferences/population (last visited July 5, 2023).

[41] *See* World Population Conf., E/CONF.41/4: Meeting 8.8. Promotion of demographic research and training in developing countries; Meeting 8.10. Population and natural resources (ex: Population growth and power resources); Meeting A. 7. Demographic aspects of agricultural development and food supply (ex: Relationship between population pressure (or growth) and systems of land tenure, the fragmentation of holdings, and customs affecting fertility in rural areas. / Population growth in relation to the agricultural labour force in and some developing American countries. / The relationship between the volume of agricultural investment and the rate of population increase).

[42] CONFERENCES | POPULATION, UN, https://www.un.org/fr/conferences/population/index (last visited July 5, 2023).

From economic concern to health concern: explaining human reproductive research

From the observation to the implementation of a solution by the WHO: the creation of the *Human Reproduction Unit*

In January 1965, in the context of the Second World Population Conference to be held that year, the Executive Board of WHO took note[43] of resolution 1048 (XXXVII) and requested the Director-General to report on activities that WHO could include in its program concerning the health aspects of the world population situation. The Director-General presented this report[44] in April 1965, and stated that "the importance of many medical, biological, social, cultural and economic factors in human reproduction made it a major public health problem."[45] This paper also mirrored the health impact of uncontrolled human reproduction on populations. Indeed, it discussed the health aspects of population dynamics, including the relationship between population trends and Health services.[46] The Director-General also emphasized the demographic control that fertility control allows: "Fertility as has long been known, can be controlled in such a fashion as either to increase or to decrease the numbers of any population. Control of fertility in man is rapidly becoming of world interest and

---

[43] WHO Executive Board Res. EB35.R31, *On Decisions of the United Nations affecting WHO's Activities: Resolution 1048 (XXXVII) of the Economic and Social Council*, (Jan. 27, 1965), 35th Sess. Geneva, 19-28 January 1965, Part I: Resolutions annexes (1965), https://apps.who.int/iris/handle/10665/88958.

[44] World Health Organization [WHO], A18/P&B/4, *Programme Activities in the Health Aspects of World Population which might be Developed by WHO, Report by the Director-General*, 18th World Health Assembly, pt. 1 annex 18, at 153-60 (Apr. 27, 1965), https://apps.who.int/iris/handle/10665/136768?search-result=true&query=A18%2FP%26B%2F4&scope=&rpp=10&sort_by=score&order=desc (referring to resolution 1048 (XXXVII) of 1964 and resolution EB35.R3).

[45] *Id.* at 1 (page numbers in these citations refer to a PDF of this report on its own, separate from the larger World Health Assembly report; the page numbers in note 44 coincide with the larger report. This will remain standard practice throughout this report).

[46] *Id.* at 8.

involves problems of both physical and mental health."[47] Finally, he felt that "WHO should be prepared to give advice, on request, to the health administrations of its Members and Associate Members on the medical aspects and treatment of sterility and the medical aspects of family planning. It should also be in a position to advise on the place such subjects should have in the health services of the community."[48]

This report of the Director-General was approved by resolution WHA18.49 of the World Health Assembly in May 1965.[49] The latter refers to Article 2.l. of the WHO Constitution, which states that in order to achieve its purpose, the Organization shall seek "to promote maternal and child health and welfare and to foster the ability to live harmoniously in a changing total environment." This resolution considered that demographic changes have an impact on health and asked the Director-General to implement the program developed in his report by producing "studies on medical aspects of sterility and fertility control methods and health aspects of population dynamics." It also asserted "that the changes in the size and structure of the population have repercussions on health conditions". Finally, noting a lack of scientific knowledge in this area, it also asked the latter to implement the advisory services it had proposed "on the under- standing that such services are related, within the responsibilities of WHO, to technical advice on the health aspects of human reproduction and should not involve operational activities." According to Egon Diczfalusy[50] in a 1985 article,[51] this is the beginning of the *Human Reproduction Unit*:

---

[47] *Id.* at 10.

[48] *Id.* at 11.

[49] World Health Organization [WHO], Res. WHA18.49, *On Programme Activities in the Health Aspects of World Population Which might be Developed by WHO,* (May 21, 1965), 18th World Health Assembly Geneva, 4-21 May 1965, Part I: Resolutions and Decisions (1965) https://apps.who.int/iris/handle/10665/89329?search-result=true&query=WHA18.49&scope=&rpp=10&sort_by=score&order=desc.

[50] Collaborator of Alexander Kessler the first director of the HRP, and senior consultant to the HRP from 1984 to 1996.

[51] E Diczfalusy, *World Health Organization Special Programme of Research, Development and Research Training in Human Reproduction. An International Response to a Global Concern,* 32 CONTRACEPTION 323, 326 (Oct. 1985), https://www.sciencedirect.com/science/article/abs/pii/0010782485900368.

"Supported by a contribution of $500,000 from the USA, the same year (1965) WHO [...] establishes a new Unit in Human Reproduction." However, while stating that "problems of human reproduction involve the family unit as well as society as a whole," Resolution WHA18.49 notes, in a way that seems contradictory, "that the size of the family should be the free choice of each individual family." It also recognizes "that it is not the responsibility of WHO to endorse or promote any particular population policy." This type of contraction can be explained by the diplomatic games that involve the drafting of consensual texts to allow most States to vote for them. In 1965, the category "human reproduction" received the first financial allocation from the WHO.[52]

The beginnings of the *Human Reproduction Unit*

After the Director-General presented his report in 1965, the President of the World Health Assembly recalled the chronology of WHO's Programme in human reproduction since 1965 when the Eighteenth World Health Assembly outlined it (Resolution WHA18.49). The President explained that it was the concern of certain governments, faced with the lack of correlation between low growth rates and the population boom, which the UN predicted would explode, that prompted WHO to take this issue into account in its work, considering it to be a problem intimately linked to family health. "In tackling from the health and human genetics point of view the somewhat controversial problem of family planning," the Health Assembly had then thought "that scientific knowledge with regard to the biology of human reproduction and the medical aspects of fertility control was insufficient." It is this observation that led the WHO to invest in these issues in the years that followed.[53]

---

[52] WHO Executive Board, EB41/WP2 - *WHO Research Programme*, 41st Sess., at 6 (Jan. 23, 1968), https://apps.who.int/iris/handle/10665/144420?search-result=true&query=%22EB41%2FWP2%22&scope=%2F&rpp=10&sort_by=score&order=desc.

[53] World Health Organization [WHO], Address by the President of the Assembly, *in* 26th World Health Assembly, Geneva, 7-23 May 1973: part II: verbatim records of plenary meetings, 60-61 (1973), https://apps.who.int/iris/handle/10665/85863.

In a 1967 report,[54] the Director-General confirmed that a *Human Reproduction Unit* had been established at WHO Headquarters in 1965. In 1966, Alexander Kessler was recruited by the WHO to head this Unit.[55] In an article from 1967, he is also presented as the chief.[56] Alexander Kessler came from *Rockefeller University* in New York, where he had conducted research on the interrelation between population dynamics and genetics.[57] In 1965, the *Human Reproduction Unit* was created within the *Family Health Division.*[58]

Conducting fertility research: WHO's population control strategy to improve health

In May 1966, the Director-General published a second report.[59] Beginning with an overview, he explained that in 1965 the WHO's *Advisory Committee on Medical Research* (ACMR) had studied the relationship between population dynamics and public health (under the headings of biological and social factors influencing population dynamics and the relationship of health services to population growth). The Committee felt that WHO should initiate and sponsor research on

---

[54] World Health Organization [WHO], A20/P&B/11,*Health Aspects of Population Dynamics: Report by the Director-General,* (May 4, 1967), *in* 20th World Health Assembly Geneva, 8-26 May 1967, Part I: Resolutions and Decisions, (1967) https://apps.who.int/iris/handle/10665/137602?search-result=true&query=A20%2FP%26B%2F11&scope=&rpp=10&sort_by=score&order=desc [hereinafter A20/P&B/11].

[55] World Health Organization, *In memory: Dr Alexander Kessler, co-founder of HRP,* (Jan. 27, 2021) https://www.who.int/news/item/27-01-2021-in-memory-dr-alexander-kessler-co-founder-of-hrp.

[56] Alexander Kessler, Ma*ternal Health and Infant Mortality, in* Proceedings of the Eighth International Conference of the International Planned Parenthood Federation, 9-15 Apr 1967: Santiago, CL, at 97 https://pdf.usaid.gov/pdf_docs/PNAAK508.pdf.

[57] *See* Alexander Kessler & Constance C. Standley, *Research on Birth Control Technology,* INTERDISC. SCI. REVS. 196, 196-201 (1978), http://dx.doi.org/10.1179/030801878791926038.

[58] Benagiano & Diczfalusy, *supra* note 6, at 370-73.

[59] World Health Organization [WHO], A19/P&B/19, *Programme Activities in the Health Aspects of World Population which might be Developed by WHO, Report by the Director-General,* (May 13, 1966), *in* 19th World Health Assembly Geneva, 3-20 May 1966, Part I: Resolutions and Decisions, annex 13 at 60-64 (1966), https://apps.who.int/iris/handle/10665/137313?search-result=true&query=A19%2FP%26B%2F19&scope=&rpp=10&sort_by=score&order=desc (referring to WHO Res. WHA18.49 and Economic & Social Council Res. 1084 (XXXIX) of 1965).

these topics, particularly in the areas of fertility, fertility control techniques, infertility and abortion. Such research should be conducted primarily in developing countries and should be linked to medical and clinical counseling programs, so as to obtain the voluntary cooperation of the population studied.[60] The Director-General also reported that several scientific groups had met this year to study, among other things, the immunological aspects of human reproduction. In this regard, he considered that this "give rise to the possibility of controlling fertility in the human being by immunization, particularly against one or more of the components of seminal fluid."[61] Taking into account resolution WHA18.49, the Director-General further considered that WHO's role in these future programs should be to advise governments, organize demonstrations, and train health personnel in the medical aspects of infertility and family planning.[62]

This report of the Director-General was approved by a resolution of the World Health Assembly in May 1966.[63] It began by "noting the part played by economic, social and cultural conditions in solving population problems, and emphasizing the importance of health aspects of this problem." It went[64] on to note that WHO has already played a role in researching and disseminating information on human reproduction but felt that scientific knowledge on this topic is not yet sufficient and that it is important to include information on the health aspects of population issues in the education of health professionals. Thus, the Health Assembly confirmed "that the role of WHO is to give

---

[60] *Id.* at 3 (see note 45 for an explanation of the difference in page numbers).
[61] *Id.* at 5.
[62] *Id.* at 9-10.
[63] World Health Organization [WHO], Res. WHA19.43, *On Programme Activities in the Health Aspects of World Population which might be Developed by WHO,* (May 20, 1966), *in* 19th World Health Assembly Geneva, 3-20 May 1966, Part I: Resolutions and Decisions (1966), https://apps.who.int/iris/handle/10665/89388?search-result=true&query=%22WHA19.43%22&scope=&rpp=10&sort_by=score&order=desc.
[64] *Id.* (referring to Economic and Social Council Res. 1084 (XXXIX) and the discussions at the Second World Population Conference).

Members technical advice, upon request, in the development of activities in family planning, as part of an organized health service."[65]

Looking back on this period, the Director-General explained several years later that "the period 1963-1968 saw the development of the WHO programme of research on demographic and biological aspects of population dynamics, including fertility control, a case in which research served as an entry to a field of activity of delicate and at that time highly- controversial nature, and allowed the Organization to play its full role on the world scene in the international handling of the matter. That programme prefigured the WHO Special Programme on Research, Development and Research Training in Human Reproduction."[66]

UN approval of the direction taken by the WHO

In September 1966, UN General Assembly resolution 2211(XXI)[67] recalled the Secretary-General's survey of governments on the problems resulting from the interaction of economic development and demographic change[68] and took note of the summary of the main discussions at the World Population Conference in Belgrade. Concerned about the difficulties of feeding a growing population in developing countries, it recognized the need to continue studies on the economic and social impact of population growth. It thus endorsed the decision of WHO to include in its programme of activities the study of

---

[65] *Id.*

[66] World Health Organization [WHO], EB63/PC/WP/7, *Programme Committee of the Executive Board: Development and Coordination of Biomedical and Health Services Research: Progress Report by the Director-General,* at 4 (1978), https://apps.who.int/iris/handle/10665/154059?search-result=true&query=EB63%2FPC%2FWP%2F7&scope=&rpp=10&sort_by=score&order=desc.

[67] United Nations: G.A. Res. 2211 (XXI), *On Population Growth and Economic Development,* (Sept. 7, 1966), https://undocs.org/Home/Mobile?FinalSymbol=a%2Fres%2F2211(XXI)&Language=E&DeviceType=Desktop&LangRequested=False (referring in particular to resolutions 1048 (XXXVII), 1084 (XXXIX), WHA18.49 and WHA19.43).

[68] After General Assembly resolution 1838 (XVII) of 1962.

the health aspects of human reproduction and the provision of advisory services.[69] Similarly, it also requested the Secretary-General to continue to implement the guidelines of resolution 1084 (XXXIX) of 1965 with regard to training and research in the population field. Finally, it called for continued consultations with the specialized agencies concerned in order to ensure effective coordination of the activities of the various United Nations agencies in the population field. Note that the General Assembly also reaffirmed the "the sovereignty of nations in formulating and promoting their own population policies, with due regard to the principle that the size of the family should be the free choice of each individual family."[70]

[69] In accordance with resolution WHA19.43.

[70] G.A. Res. 2211(XXI), *supra* note 67.

Chapter 3
Fertility regulation for better overall health

Addressing health issues caused by population growth

On May 4, 1967, the Director-General of WHO issued his first report[71] on the health aspects of population dynamics.[72] There, the Director-General outlined WHO's activities related to this issue. The study of human reproduction, which he recalled has been an active issue for WHO since 1963, was one of them. According to the Director-General, the increase in population negatively influences its general health status by putting pressure on health services. This implies training more health personnel. On the other hand, advances in medicine and technology reduce the mortality rate and can reinforce population growth. This is a problem when a portion of the population can no longer access resources: "Imbalance between economic, educational, social, cultural, and health resources on the one hand and population numbers on the other hand, become problems when they affect the standard of living and the quality of life."[73] This report was approved by a resolution of the Health Assembly in 1967.[74] This one began by "considering that abortions and the high maternal and child mortality rates constitute a serious public health problem in many countries" and that the development of basic health services should be the foundation of any program to address the health problems posed by population growth. It requested the Director-General to continue to develop WHO's activities in the field of human reproductive health and to help

---

[71] A20/P&B/11, *supra* note 54.

[72] In accordance with World Health Assembly resolution WHA19.43 of 1966.

[73] A20/P&B/11, *supra* note 54, at 2.

World Health Organization [WHO], Res. WHA20.41, *On Health Aspects of Population Dynamics,* (May 25, 1967), *in* 20th World Health Assembly Geneva, 8-26 May 1967 Part I: Resolutions and Decisions, (1967), https://apps.who.int/iris/handle/10665/89508?search-result=true&query=WHA20.41&scope=&rpp=10&sort_by=score&order=desc (referring to and reaffirming the considerations developed in Resolutions WHA18.49 and WHA19.43).

with the implementation of national research projects and for the training of personnel.

On April 24, 1968, the Director-General issued his second report on the health aspects of population dynamics.[75] It was approved by a resolution of the World Health Assembly in May 1968.[76] The resolution expressed satisfaction with the increasing demands[77] for research and professional training and advisory services to Member States on the health aspects of human reproduction, family planning, and population dynamics. The resolution also requested that the Director-General continue his action in this direction. Additionally, the Health Assembly also emphasized that these problems must be solved by taking into consideration economic, social, cultural, psychological and health factors. It also recognized that despite their importance to families; knowledge about the health aspects of human reproduction, family planning, and population is still limited. The Health Assembly therefore requested the Director-General to expand WHO's program in this area, particularly by encouraging research on psychological factors related to the health aspects of human reproduction. It also invited him to expand the training of health personnel on these issues.

In accordance with the 1968 resolution,[78] on June 5, 1969, the Director-General of WHO issued his third report[79] on the health aspects of

---

[75] World Health Organization [WHO], A21/P&B/9,*Health Aspects of Population Dynamics: Report by the Director-General,* (Apr. 24, 1968), *in* 21st World Health Assembly, Geneva, 6-24 May 1968, Part I: Resolutions and Decisions (1968) https://apps.who.int/iris/handle/10665/143495?search-result=true&query=A21%2FP%26B%2F9&scope=%2F&rpp=10&sort_by=score&order=desc [hereinafter A21/P&B/9] (in accordance with resolution WHA20.41).

[76] World Health Organization [WHO], Res. WHA21.43, *On Health Aspects of Population Dynamics,* (May 23, 1968), *in* 21st World Health Assembly Geneva, 6-24 May 1968, Part I: Resolutions and Decisions, (1968), https://apps.who.int/iris/handle/10665/91192?search-result=true&query=WHA21.43&scope=&rpp=10&sort_by=score&order=desc.

[77] In Res. WHA18.49, WHA19.43, and WHA20.41.

[78] WHA21.43, *supra* note 76.

[79] World Health Organization [WHO], A22/P&B/11, *Health Aspects of Population Dynamics: Progress Report by the Director-General,* 22d World Health Assembly, Geneva,

population dynamics. This report was approved by a resolution of the World Health Assembly in May 1969.[80] In this resolution, it expressed its satisfaction with the progress of the program activities on the health aspects of human reproduction, family planning and population dynamics.[81] It requested the Director-General to continue the program of advisory services in support of training and research. It also asked him to study how to implement "services for family planning care specifically in the context of health services and generally in the context of community, economic and national development." Finally, it requested the Director-General to intensify the development of basic health services as a means of meeting family planning needs.

Finally, in 1971, the Director-General presented his annual report to the World Health Assembly and the United Nations. Part of this report dealt with human reproduction in the chapter "Family Health."[82]

These four reports of the Director-General highlighted four roles that WHO had taken on in its response to the health challenges caused by population growth. That is to say its advisory and coordinating roles; and driving roles in documentary and biomedical research; and in the training of medical personnel.

8-25 July 1969, Part I: Resolutions and Decisions, (1969), https://apps.who.int/iris/handle/10665/144295?search-result=true&query=A22%2FP%26B%2F11&scope=&rpp=10&sort_by=score&order=desc [hereinafter A22/P&B/11].

[80] World Health Organization [WHO], Res. WHA22.32, *On Health Aspects of Population Dynamics*, (July 23, 1969), *in* 22d World Health Assembly, Geneva, 8-25 July 1969, Part I: Resolutions and Decisions, at 13-14 (July 23, 1969), https://apps.who.int/iris/handle/10665/91257?search-result=true&query=WHA22.32&scope=&rpp=10&sort_by=score&order=desc.

[81] In accordance with previous resolutions WHA18.49, WHA19.43, WHA20.41 and WHA21.43

[82] World Health Organization [WHO], *The Work of WHO 1970, Annual Report of the Director-General to the World Health Assembly and to the United Nations*, 74-76 (1971) https://apps.who.int/iris/handle/10665/85828 [hereinafter *Work of WHO 1970*].

The four roles taken by the WHO in the face of health challenges caused by population growth

WHO's advisory role in promoting family planning as a response to the health challenges of population growth

In his 1967 report,[83] the Director-General of WHO referred to resolution WHA19.43 of 1966. Together with resolution WHA18.49, this resolution defined WHO's program, particularly regarding the conditions under which the organization could provide advisory services to Member States on population matters. This issue was well taken care of, for in 1968 the Director-General stated that WHO had provided advisory support to Member States that had requested it in the development of programs concerning the health aspects of family planning and had continued its work, particularly in research in this area.[84] It also expected to receive an increasing number of requests for advisory support from member states. However, the Director-General recalled that "WHO does not endorse or promote any particular population policy, [and] recognizes that the problems of human reproduction involve the family unit as well as society, and that the size of the family is the free choice of each individual family."[85]

The advisory services proposed by WHO were based on the observation that countries tend to allocate their limited resources in the best possible way, particularly in the field of health services. "Better health is correlated with changes from wasteful patterns of high mortality and high natality to more productive patterns of low mortality, with natality regulated as desired - whether this involves an increase or decrease over previous levels."[86] The objective was to raise the level of health care through the establishment of appropriate infrastructures. The Director-General considered that "a minimal level

---

[83] A20/P&B/11, *supra* note 54.

[84] In accordance with resolutions WHA18.49 of 1965, WHA19.43 of 1966, and WHA20.41 of 1967.

[85] A21/P&B/9, *supra* note 75,at 2.

[86] *Id.* at 1.

of health sems to be necessary for a family to realize that it can regulate its own "demographic" behaviour."[87] Understood in this sense, health services were a mechanism that WHO considered important in determining demographic trends. The increased standard of living that higher health status would bring would enhance the value of individuals and be "fundamental to the development of populations as positive resources," because it considered an unhealthy population "incapable of participating in the social, intellectual, economic and technological development of a country."[88]

On October 3, 1969, a resolution of the WHO Regional Committee for Southeast Asia on the health aspects of population dynamics was issued.[89] The resolution assumed that the best way to provide family planning programs was through general health services. This was because it considered "that only the increasing assurance of child survival and family welfare will induce parents to accept the small family norm." The Regional Committee then asked the Regional Director to provide assistance to governments that requested it in the area of family planning within the framework of health services and training of health personnel. It also asked him to work in this field in collaboration with other United Nations organizations and to transmit to the WHO Director-General any request for research assistance in this field from the governments of the region.

In 1970, the Director-General noted the growing demand for assistance from Member States "concerning human reproduction, family planning and population dynamics." Particularly with grants from the United Nations Fund for Population Activities and the Swedish International

---

[87] *Id.*

[88] *Id.*

[89] WHO & Reg'l Comm. Se. Asia, Res. SEA/RC22/R7, *On Health Aspects of Population Dynamics* (Oct. 3, 1969), https://apps.who.int/iris/handle/10665/130244?search-result=true&query=SEA%2FRC22%2FR7&scope=&rpp=10&sort_by=score&order=desc. Referring to resolutions WHA18.45 (Probably a mistake, the correct reference staying within the theme is WHA18.49) of 1965, WHA19.43 of 1966, WHA20.41 of 1967, WHA21.43 of 1968 and WHA22.32 of 1969.

Development Cooperation Agency, WHO was able to respond and continue to provide advisory services on the development of family planning services integrated with the health infrastructure.[90]

WHO's coordinating role

Article 70 of the WHO Constitution[91] states that "the Organization shall establish effective relations and co-operate closely with such other inter-governmental organizations as may be desirable. Any formal agreement entered into with such organizations shall be subject to approval by a two-thirds vote of the Health Assembly." Similarly, section 71 provides that "the Organization may, on matters within its competence, make suitable arrangements for consultation and co-operation with non-governmental international organizations and, with the consent of the Government concerned, with national organizations, governmental or non-governmental."

In 1968, the Director-General ensured the best possible coordination between WHO and other UN agencies[92] in its work on population. In particular, the Organization coordinated with the United Nations Population Division and Statistical Office, the United Nations Children's Fund (UNICEF), and the International Labour Organization (ILO). WHO was also advising UNESCO on the role it could play in the field of population. WHO had also attended the third and fourth sessions of the *Administrative Committee on Coordination* (ACC) inter-agency meeting on population programs.[93] Coordination with the United Nations Organizations thus remained an important point in a

---

[90] *Work of WHO 1970, supra* note 82.

[91] WHO, *Constitution of the World Health Organization, in* BASIC DOCUMENTS, (49th ed., 2020) https://apps.who.int/gb/bd/pdf_files/BD_49th-en.pdf#page=6.

[92] A21/P&B/9, *supra* note 75.

[93] The *Administrative Committee on Coordination* (ACC) is the only body that brings together the executive heads of all the organizations of the United Nations system, under the chairmanship of the Secretary-General. *See* Francesco Messalama, Khalil Issa Othman, & Louis-Dominique Ouedraogo, *Review of the Administrative Coordinating Committee and its Mechanisms*, at 5 (1999), https://www.unjiu.org/sites/www.unjiu.org/files/jiu_document_files/products/fr/reports-notes/JIU%20Products/JIU_REP_1999_01_French.pdf.

period where "their mandates are being broadened, projects are in a phase of active development, and coordination of programmes is being promoted towards common objectives"[94] particularly regarding family planning. Thus, the ACC decided to keep abreast of developments in population issues so that the actions of UN organizations could be as effective as possible. The WHO also maintained links with NGOs, private organizations, foundations and educational institutions that were interested in the health aspects of human reproduction, family planning and population dynamics. The Director-General had announced what appears to be the first collaboration between *Karolinska Institute* and WHO to conduct various methodological work related to reproduction.[95] In 1970, the Organization designated the Research Unit on Reproductive Endocrinology of the *Karolinska Institute*[96] in Stockholm as the WHO *Research and Training Centre* for Human Reproduction. It was planned that his work would focus on pharmacologically regulated reproductive processes and on the training of researchers in this field.[97]

In 1970, cooperation among agencies and organizations remained important to WHO. For example, the Director-General felt that UNESCO could be concerned with educational projects related to human reproduction in youth programs and in the school sector. In 1970, WHO also participated in the work of the *Subcommittee on Population* of the *Administrative Committee on Coordination* (ACC) and the *United Nations Fund for Population Activities* (UNFPA). She was also represented at a meeting on social development and family planning

---

[94] A22/P&B/11, *supra* note 79, at 5.
[95] *Id.*
[96] Professor Diczfalusy was the director of this unit, which is why he was appointed "Senior Consultant" of the HRP from the beginning. Egon Diczfalusy, CURRICULUM VITAE, DICZFALUSY FOUNDATION, https://diczfalusyfoundation.org/egon-diczfalusy/cv (last visited July 4, 2023).
[97] *Work of WHO 1970, supra* note 82.

organized in the United Kingdom by the *International Planned Parenthood Federation* (IPPF).[98]

The beginnings of documentary and biomedical research undertaken under the aegis of the WHO through the creation of international reference research centers

In 1967, the Director-General noted in his report[99] that the role of the *Human Reproduction Unit* was to provide a clearinghouse for information on human reproduction, to encourage, coordinate, and support scientific research in this field, and to provide advisory services to Member States on medical problems of fertility, infertility, and methods of fertility regulation.[100] In order to establish this documentation center, ten expert meetings were held at WHO headquarters between 1963 and 1966. Among the different subjects treated, we can note the immunological aspects of human reproduction and the study of intrauterine devices.[101] A Scientific Group on the Biology of Birth Regulation by Periodic Continence was also convened in June 1966. The *Human Reproduction Unit* had also compiled a bibliography of publications on human reproduction since 1942 and critically reviewed them. Similarly, it had also identified institutions and researchers working on human reproductive issues. Thus, it continuously collected data on issues related to the health aspects of population dynamics, including issues related to fertility, infertility, and the incidence of abortion. Within the framework of the research of the *Human Reproduction Unit,* work was carried out, for example, on steroid hormones for the design of male contraceptives and on the clinical and serological aspects of spermatic auto-antibodies in men.[102] The Twentieth World Health Assembly having considered in 1967 "that abortions and the high maternal and child mortality rates constitute a serious public health problem in many countries" (resolution

---

[98] *Id.*

[99] A20/P&B/11, *supra* note 54.

[100] *Id.* at 4-5.

[101] *Id.* at 5.

[102] *Id.* at 7.

WHA20.41), the Organization undertook a study of how spontaneous and induced abortion, as well as its causes and consequences, were defined and recorded by Member States. Various epidemiological methods for assessing the frequency of induced abortion and its health impact were being developed. Epidemiological studies on human reproduction had been carried out and the Director-General had announced the Organization's support for a prospective study on abortion in São Paulo, Brazil, which consisted of following a sample of women through periodic interviews.[103]

In 1968, the Director-General reported that WHO had continued its documentation work with the *Human Reproduction Unit,* with bibliographic work on topics including the health aspects of family planning, fertility regulation, contraception and abortion. A scientific group had also continued to work on contraception using hormonal steroids and on the development of new contraceptives, particularly injectable preparations. Another group also reviewed the state of knowledge of the time on the effects of contraception with intrauterine devices (physiological and clinical considerations). The Organization also supported field research projects to determine the best ways to organize family planning and the training of health personnel. Also in the area of scientific research, the Director-General reported that WHO continued to support the prospective study on abortion in Brazil and was interested in conducting similar studies. It should be noted that the Director-General, recognizing that science still lacked knowledge about certain processes of reproduction and fetal development, considered that it was difficult to evaluate "some of the biological effects being produced by currently available methods of fertility regulation." However, while he recognized the existence of risks, he felt that they were less significant than the "potential hazards of maternal morbidity and mortality secondary to unwanted pregnancies and abortion." He thus called for more research in the field.[104]

---

[103] *Id.* at 7.

[104] A21/P&B/9, *supra* note 75.

In 1969, the Director-General noted that WHO also continued to "stimulate, co[]ordinate and support research in the biomedical aspects of human reproduction and of family planning." The mechanisms put in place by the WHO for this "were extended, as already mentioned, to epidemiological and service research."[105] This year, WHO had also initiated the creation of international reference research centers on human reproduction to promote the training of researchers. WHO considered the establishment of such centers "planned for the evaluation of different methods of fertility control, on the morbidity associated with spontaneous and induced abortion, and on standardization of fertility promoting substances." WHO had also continued the periodic evaluation of fertility control agents. In the same logic, another project aimed "to assess the impact of intensive childcare on acceptance of family planning. It examines the hypothesis that parents will be more willing to space and limit family size with an assurance of child survival."[106] As a result of the study begun in 1967 on spontaneous and induced abortion, the Director-General reported that these problems were to be studied later this year (1969) by a scientific panel on unproductive pregnancies and maternal morbidity and mortality as related to spontaneous and induced abortion.[107]

In 1970, work also continued by WHO scientific panels on the endocrine regulation of human gestation and on advances in research and clinical experience with fertility regulation methods. These scientific panels especially reviewed developments in the safety and efficacy of hormonal steroids and intrauterine devices. The issue of implementation and cost of clinical trials of new fertility regulating agents was a point of concern for the WHO. A study was also conducted with the participation of centers in different countries (India, Iran, Lebanon, Pakistan, Philippines, Taiwan, and Turkey) to determine the impact that family size and growth rate could have on family health.

---

[105] A22/P&B/11, *supra* note 79, at 4.

[106] *Id.* at 3-4.

[107] *Id.* at 5-6.

Other epidemiological surveys had also been supported by WHO in the field of family planning in India, Nigeria, and Peru.[108]

WHO's involvement in the training of medical personnel and the implementation of family planning

In 1968, in addition to the role that family planning should play in solving demographic problems, the Director-General noted that States saw family planning as an important element in the medical protection of mothers and children and in the improvement of family health. He considered that family planning should be able to deal with various problems related to reproduction: subfertility, sterility, abortion, pregnancy, sexual education, and contraception. This meant training staff and increasing research in these areas (effectiveness and safety of contraceptives; diagnosis and treatment of infertility; health aspects of the problem of spontaneous or induced abortion, etc.) and on how to implement responses: "The consideration of the pertinent social and cultural factors that affect reproductive health and disease form important components of advice in these areas."[109]

In 1969, the Director-General noted that the Organization had continued to support family planning education and professional training by intensifying its work in this area.[110] WHO also took care to improve the training of its staff so that they could best respond to the increasing requests for advice from member states on family planning. In fact, in 1969, the Organization had projects underway in the following countries: the Central African Republic, Gabon, Costa Rica, El Salvador, Honduras, Nicaragua, Trinidad, Tobago, Ecuador, Haiti, Colombia, Guatemala, Peru, Pakistan, United Arab Republic, Algeria, Turkey, India, Indonesia, Nepal, Thailand, Republic of Korea, Malaysia, Singapore, and Western Samoa. It also appears, as explained by the Director-General, that "Regional advisers [...]are giving attention to the

---

108 *Work of WHO 1970, supra* note 82.

109 A21/P&B/9, *supra* note 75, at 2.

110 A22/P&B/11, *supra* note 79, at 4.

family planning component of services in countries where this is a Government priority programme already included in the health structure."[111] This appears to be a direct action by WHO that can be interpreted as contrary to, or at least as a change from, resolution WHA18.49 of 1965, which stated that WHO's services in this area should not include operational activities.

In July 1969, the WHO Regional Director for the Western Pacific issued a report.[112] He was referring to resolution WP/RC19.R8 of the WHO Regional Committee for South-East Asia, which requested him to develop this area in the health programs in the region. In response to this request, the Regional Director had focused on training his staff through WHO headquarters and on training medical staff in the region in general. It is also reported that the Government of Singapore, WHO, and UNICEF, had signed a partnership in late 1968 for a project on maternal and child health and family planning services. This report was endorsed by Resolution WRP/RC20.R7[113] of the WHO Regional Committee for Southeast Asia on September 29, 1969. This Resolution urged the Regional Director to seek ways to develop other family planning activities that might be requested by governments. The Committee also endorsed efforts to promote family planning activities as part of basic health service programs while hoping that WHO might benefit from financial assistance from the *United Nations Trust Fund for Population Activities* (UNFPA).

In 1970, the Director-General reported that WHO was still providing assistance for training and research (Indonesia and Taiwan). WHO was also continuing its reflection on the most effective means of

---

[111] *Id.* at 3.
[112] WHO & Reg'l Comm. W. Pac., WRP/RC20/5, *Health Aspects of Population Dynamics: Report by the Regional Director*, (July 14, 1969), https://apps.who.int/iris/handle/10665/139174?search-result=true&query=Health+aspects+of+population+dynamics%3A+report+by+the+Director-General&scope=%2F&rpp=10&sort_by=score&order=desc.
[113] WHO & Reg'l Comm. W. Pac., Res. WRP/RC20.R7, *On Health Aspects of Population Dynamics* (Sept. 29, 1969), https://apps.who.int/iris/handle/10665/358042?search-result=true&query=WPR%2FRC20.R7&scope=&rpp=10&sort_by=score&order=desc

implementation in these areas with the organization of meetings and seminars in different countries (India, Iraq, and Iran). In response to requests from States, in 1970 the staff training program was also reoriented towards national health personnel, even though WHO had continued, since 1969, to train its own staff, those of the regional offices (in India, the United Arab Republic, and the Republic of Korea) and its operational staff in the Western Pacific Region (in which agents from UNICEF and UNESCO had also participated). For example, a two-month course for obstetricians and gynecologists was held with WHO support at the Indian Central Family Planning Institute in New Delhi; and a guide to facilitate training was prepared. With the same objective, a study group meeting in Geneva also discussed and defined objectives for the development of public education in family planning.[114]

---

[114] *Work of WHO 1970, supra* note 82.

PART TWO

The establishment of a Special Programme on Human Reproduction: a response to demographic concerns through the development of contraceptives

In 1968, Paul R. Ehrlich published the book *The Population Bomb*.[115] The catastrophist thesis of the book was that the growth of the world's population would cause famine in the 1970s and 1980s, resulting in the death of hundreds of million people, or even the collapse of humanity in a thermonuclear war, unless measures were taken to limit population growth. The book was a great success and sold over two million copies.

According to two former HRP administrators, G. Benagiano and E. Diczfalusy,[116] "while in the early 1960s only 7 governments provided family planning programmes, by the early 1980s over 120 governments supported such programmes."[117] For them it was the evolution of ideas about human reproduction that led to the creation of a new institutional framework:

---

[115] PAUL R. EHRLICH, THE POPULATION BOMB, (Ballantine Books, 1968), http://pinguet.free.fr/ehrlich68.pdf.
[116] G. Benagiano was Director of the HRP, unlike Professor Diczfalusy who was never a member of the WHO. He was Senior Consultant for the HRP.
[117] Benagiano & Diczfalusy, *supra* note 6, at 371.

The major milestones in the creation of new institutions in this area were: (I) the establishment of the International Planned Parenthood Federation in Bombay (1952); (II) the creation of the Population Council in New York (1952); (II) the initiation of the Ford Foundation's global programme to support research and research training in human reproduction (1958); (IV) the call, [...] by the General Assembly of the United Nations in 1962, for the entire United Nations system to develop facilities for training, research, information and advisory services in the population field; (V) the establishment by the World Health Organization of the Human Reproduction Unit within the Family Health Division in 1965, as a response to resolution WHA18.48 [...] (VI) the coming into being in 1967 of the United Nations Population Trust Fund, forerunner of the [...] United Nations Population Fund (UNFPA); (VII) the Teheran Proclamation of the United Nations Conference on Human Rights, which affirmed that information on and access to family planning are basic human rights; (VIII) the creation in 1972 by the WHO of the Special Programme of Research, Development and Research Training in Human Reproduction; (IX) the expansion of the support, in 1988, for the Special Programme which became an Inter-Agency Programme of the United Nations and is co-sponsored by the United Nations Development Programme (UNDP), the United Nations Population Fund (UNFPA), the World Bank and the WHO, the latter being the executing agency.[118]

[118] *Id.* at 372.

Chapter 4
The creation of the Programme and its objectives

G. Benagiano and E. Diczfalusy also mention the creation of the Programme:

> How was the Special Programme created? By the end of 1969 the Swedish International Development Authority (SIDA), strongly supported by the Ford and Rockefeller Foundations, had advanced plans for the establishment of the Agency for Contraceptive Research and Development (ACORD) at the Karolinska Institute in Stockholm in order to stimulate and promote international research in the field. In early 1970, however, the plans were abandoned when the government of a former 'superpower' was found to be unsympathetic to the idea. In June 1970, a number of interested agencies met at the WHO in Geneva to consider a global research programme on human reproduction. Before embarking on such a worldwide endeavour, the WHO wished to conduct a 'feasibility study'; the idea appealed very much to the agencies and SIDA provided the necessary financial means. At this point, the genius of Or A. Kessler, the first Director of the Programme, made its initial impact; within a few months consultants and staff visited 69 institutions in 23 countries and a full-scale report (proposing a 'Five Track Programme') was published. [...] What was the original aim of the 'Five Track Programme'? The establishment of four regional research and training centres; a network of clinical research centres; a dozen or so multinational, multidisciplinary

task forces; and a system of support for research resources mainly in developing countries was recommended.[119]

In 1972, Alexander Kessler, head of the *Human Reproduction Unit*, co-published a paper on the Expanded Programme.[120] He explained that this programme project was part of WHO's reproductive research programme, under its mandate, and represented a very significant investment in terms of both scope and scale of research. He also recalled that since the 1960s, WHO had been conducting research on various aspects of reproduction (fertility regulation, birth control methods, infertility treatment). This research had been developed, in particular with the support of the *Advisory Committee on Medical Research* and the *World Health Assembly*, along two lines. On the one hand, research on the biomedical aspects of reproduction; and on the other hand, epidemiological and administrative research, of which the development of family planning was an angle. Special contributions from Member States and Foundations made it possible to finance the Programme. Alexander Kessler stated the objective of the Expanded Programme, which was to improve the understanding of human reproductive processes in order to develop a variety of safe, acceptable, and effective methods of regulating human reproduction.

Feasibility study and draft research programme on reproduction and fertility regulation

It was in the context of WHO's desire to coordinate research efforts that the Expanded Programme was born after the Organization convened a meeting in June 1970 in Geneva with organizations interested in this cooperation in the field of human reproduction and more specifically in the "promotion of research in reproductive biomedicine including fertility regulation." The objective of the meeting was to discuss how

---

[119] *Id.*

[120] A. Kessler, G. W. Perkin, & C. C. Standley, HR/71.9, *in* WHO Chronicle, at 102-106 (Jan. 1972), https://apps.who.int/iris/handle/10665/361191 (at 46-55 in URL document) [hereinafter *HR/71.9*].

best to develop research and research training in this area.[121] In his annual report to the World Health Assembly and the United Nations for the year 1970,[122] The Director-General also reported on a meeting to take stock of support for research on reproductive issues, including fertility regulation. This meeting was held with representatives of national medical research councils, bilateral aid agencies, private foundations, and the International Bank for Reconstruction and Development. The urgent need to develop research and training in existing institutions was stressed.[123]

Three conclusions were drawn from this meeting. First, that the state of research was not yet sufficiently advanced; second, that more research was needed to develop family planning technology (to find new methods of fertility control); and third, that there was insufficient research support in this field. It was recommended that a feasibility study be conducted to establish a planning strategy for the development of human reproductive research and an implementation framework. This study was initiated by WHO in September and funded by the Swedish International Development Cooperation Agency and the Ford Foundation.[124] Alexander Kessler noted that WHO was assisted by a consultant from the Ford Foundation who played an active and important role in developing the Expanded Programme. The Swedish International Development Cooperation Agency (SIDA), which was one of the agencies present, provided funds to make the study possible.[125]

---

[121] World Health Organization [WHO], HR/71.4, *Expanded Programme of Research, Development and Research Training in Human Reproduction: Report of a Feasibility Project*; pt. 1 (1971), https://apps.who.int/iris/bitstream/handle/10665/361192/HR-71.4-Pt1-eng.pdf?sequence=1&isAllowed=y [hereinafter HR/71.4 pt. 1].

[122] *Work of WHO 1970, supra* note 82.

[123] World Health Organization [WHO], *The Work of WHO 1971, Annual Report of the Director-General to the World Health Assembly and to the United Nations, 1972 - Human reproduction*, § 8.29 at 132-136 (1972), https://apps.who.int/iris/handle/10665/85845 [hereinafter *Work of WHO 1971*].

[124] *Id.*

[125] *HR/71.9, supra* note 120.

The Report of Feasibility Study on an Expanded Programme of Research, Development and Research Training in Human Reproduction[126] was published in May 1971. It reported that between November 1970 and April 1971, teams of experts had visited more than 69 institutions in 23 countries to review the level and quality of research in the field of human reproduction and to assess ways to expand and accelerate the level of activities.[127] Following these expert consultations, the Secretariat developed from their reports and recommendations a proposal outlining an *Expanded Programme of Research, Development and Research Training in Human Reproduction.*[128] This five-track programme then presented a comprehensive plan of action "that would implement WHO's mandate to stimulate and expand research in human reproduction including fertility control."[129] WHO believed that it could effectively foster international scientific collaboration by mobilizing talent that would allow for significant growth in research and training in this area in complementarity with other agencies and institutions involved in this field.[130]

Five tracks for the development of the human reproduction research programme

Research and Training Centres

The first track of the Programme was the designation by WHO of at least four major *Research and Training Centres* that were to become WHO centres. Their purpose was to build momentum in human reproductive research, particularly in the regions of the world where they were located. They were also to initiate research collaboration, provide research training, organize scientific conferences, serve as regional

---

[126] HR/71.4 pt. 1, *supra* note 121.
[127] *See* World Health Organization [WHO], HR/71.4, *Expanded Programme of Research, Development and Research Training in Human Reproduction Appendices: Report of a Feasibility Project*; pt. 2 app. A at 1 (1971), https://apps.who.int/iris/bitstream/handle/10665/361192/HR-71.4-Pt2-eng.pdf?sequence=2&isAllowed=y [hereinafter HR/71.4 pt. 2].
[128] *Work of WHO 1971, supra* note 123.
[129] HR/71.4 pt. 1, *supra* note 121, at 1.
[130] *Id.*

documentation centers, and advise WHO on these issues. WHO was to provide additional financial support to these centers.[131] Two initial proposals were made in 1971. These proposals were reviewed by the Programme's *Advisory Group*, which recommended a course of action to WHO (subject to the availability of funds).[132] The first proposal was the major expansion of the WHO *Research and Training Centre* at the *Karolinska Institute.* The total projected research budget for the center was then \$6.5 million over five years, with, for example, a projected budget of \$1.4 million for a steroid research laboratory and \$120,000 for a contraceptive testing unit. Construction of the expanded 2,500 m2 Research and Training Centre building was estimated at \$2.1 million (Table 14). A second expansion proposal was also made for the *Centro Latino Americano de Biologia de la Reproduccion* (CLABIR).[133] In 1972, the four institutions chosen to be WHO *Research and Training Centres* were all selected. They were the following organizations: *All-India Institute of Medical Sciences,* New Delhi; *All Union Scientific Institute of Obstetrics and Gynaecology,* Moscow; five institutions grouped in the multinational "Three Nations Programme" center in Buenos Aires, Montevideo, and Santiago; and *Karolinska Institute and Hospital,* Stockholm.[134]

Clinical Research Centres

The track avenue for the new WHO Expanded Programme was a collaboration with clinical centers to "facilitate the rapid clinical evaluation of new fertility regulating agents." It was thus proposed to establish a global network of at least 34 collaborating clinical centers in 25 countries.[135]

---

[131] *Id.* at 2.

[132] *See also* HR/71.4 pt. 2, *supra* note 127127, app. B at 116.

[133] *Id.* at 133-146.

[134] World Health Organization [WHO], *Expanded Programme of Research, Development and Research Training in Human Reproduction: Report on Programme Implementation during the First Year, October 1972,* HR/72.5a (1972), https://apps.who.int/iris/handle/10665/361194 [hereinafter HR/72.5a].

[135] *See also* HR/71.4 pt. 2, *supra* note 127, app. C at 196.

Task forces

The third track was the establishment of *Task forces* for collaborative research and development in the field of fertility regulation. It was envisioned that it would be the role of the *Advisory Group* to set the direction of their work. The various *Task forces* were to report regularly to WHO and publish their findings. The objective was to provide a flexible mechanism through the formation of groups, which through their focused work, would aim "to accelerate the development and critical assessment of new agents affecting fertility."[136] In particular, it was planned to study prostaglandins (hormones used to induce abortion: misoprostol is a prostaglandin),[137] male contraception, comparative trials of copper IUDs, and various fertility-promoting agents.[138] In 1980, we learned that *Steering Committees* had been created to develop the strategies to be implemented in the twelve *Task Forces.*[139]

An international documentation centre on human reproduction

The fourth track was the creation by WHO of an international documentation centre on the biomedical aspects of human reproduction.[140] The aim was to create a special file for the whole field of human reproduction by indexing in the best possible way the 20,000 publications related to the biomedical aspects of human reproduction that appeared every year. For this purpose, the *Karolinska Institute* proposed to create a special unit within its biomedical documentation centre that would be in charge of compiling and maintaining as

---

[136] HR/71.4 pt. 1, *supra* note 121, at 3.

[137] "These studies aimed at using an 'antihormone' (Selective progesterone receptor modulator) followed by a prostaglandin (a hormone-like substance)". G. Benagiano. E-mail from G. Benagiano, Director of HRP 1993-97, to Louis-Marie Bonneau, ECLJ (Jan. 25, 2023 15:59 CEST) (on file with recipient).

[138] *See also* HR/71.4 pt. 2, *supra* note 127, app. D at 201.

[139] World Health Organization [WHO], A33/9, *Development and Coordination of Biomedical and Health Services Research: Progress Report by the Director-General,* § 7 at 21 (1980), https://apps.who.int/iris/handle/10665/154539?search-result=true&query=%22A33%2F9 %22&scope=%2F&rpp=10&sort_by=score&order=desc [hereinafter A33/9].

[140] *See also* HR/71.4 pt. 2, *supra* note 127, app. E at 206.

complete a file as possible on these publications, extending it to other relevant fields (chemistry, biochemistry, toxicology, immunology...).[141] This point was not followed up due to a lack of funds.[142]

Secondary tracks

The fifth track for supporting the *Expanded Human Reproduction Programme* consisted of several secondary proposals. First, there was a desire to expand support to scientists and institutions eligible for research grants and contracts. The means by which they were to receive support are described in Annex G of the document. WHO was also willing to provide equipment and reagents directly to laboratories. It also offered grants to train researchers.[143] WHO also envisioned that the network of WHO centers could increase the exchange of scientific information through a series of seminars and workshops. Finally, WHO considered the use of consultants to assist a number of developing laboratories.[144]

This five tracks programme was "endorsed by scientists and research administrators as an appropriate mechanism to accelerate the development of new fertility regulating agents and to expand research and training in this field" in August 1971.[145] WHO also planned to continue its relationship with the pharmaceutical industry in order to develop fertility regulating agents, the Expanded Programme in particular could then be available to undertake clinical trials.[146] WHO also had to present a specific program for the implementation of these tracks.[147] The goal of the Programme was that improved understanding of the human reproductive process would lead to the development of a

---

[141] HR/71.4 pt. 1, *supra* note 121, at 4.
[142] Benagiano & Diczfalusy, *supra* note 6, at 370-73.
[143] HR/71.4 pt. 1, *supra* note 121, at 5.
[144] *Id.* at 6.
[145] World Health Organization [WHO], HR/71.4, *Expanded Programme of Research, Development and Research Training in Hunan Reproduction: Report of a Feasibility Project - Supplementary Information*, add. 1 at 1 (Aug. 1971), https://apps.who.int/iris/handle/10665/361193 [hereinafter HR/71.4 add. 1].
[146] HR/71.4 pt. 1, *supra* note 121, at 7.
[147] *Id.* at 11.

variety of safe, acceptable and effective methods for the regulation of human fertility.[148] As a result of a number of additional consultations, five additional program implementation elements were proposed. These elements were both organizational and financial.[149]

In 1972, the Director-General explained[150] that for him the regulation of human fertility and its problems could only be achieved by a considerable intensification of clinical research and research efforts in three other areas: physiology, epidemiology, and public health. Thus, he informed us that the Programme had been approved in June 1971 by the *Advisory Committee on Medical Research* and that it was subsequently approved in September 1971 at a meeting attended by most of the institutions that had recommended in 1970 that WHO undertake the feasibility study. He also reported that the recommendations of the *Advisory Group* that defined the priorities for the implementation of the Programme had thus been retained. The Director-General also confirmed the five tracks of the Expanded Programme.[151]

The operational structure of the Programme

The history of governance and structure from 1970 onwards

It was planned in 1971 that the Expanded Programme would be implemented and administered within the framework of WHO policies

---

[148] HR/71.4 add. 1, *supra* note 145, at 3.

[149] *Id.*

[150] *Work of WHO 1971, supra* note 123.

[151] *Id.* at § 8.30, "The designation of a small number of existing centres as WHO research and training centres in human reproduction - in addition to that already designated in Stockholm - to conduct research with emphasis on reproductive processes susceptible to regulation and to train scientists in reproductive biomedicine; the setting up of a world - wide network of clinical collaborating centres, to evaluate new fertility - regulating agents and to undertake comparative trials of existing agents; the establishment of groups of scientists, known as "task forces", to provide collaborative research on specified problems; the creation of an international documentation centre, to compile and maintain a complete file of references to all published material on the biomedical aspects of human reproduction; and, finally, the expansion of existing programmes for, inter alia, research, training awards, and the provision of supplies and reagents for laboratory work."

and procedures, and more specifically by the *Human Reproduction Unit*, whose technical staff would be increased for this purpose, in order to cope with the increased workload involved in the Expanded Programme.[152] It was thus proposed, subject to the availability of funds, to create at least ten posts, ranging from doctors and scientists to administrative and technical staff.[153] In 1971, Dr. Alexander Kessler was still head of the *Human Reproduction Unit* of the WHO.[154] It was then planned that he would focus primarily on the Programme. Other WHO Units and Divisions were also to provide technical and administrative resources to the Programme.[155]

The report on the implementation of the Expanded Programme during the first year published in October 1972[156] highlights that in the governance of the programme, cooperation remained an important issue. Thus, in an effort to avoid duplication, contacts between WHO and the directors of these other research programs related to contraceptive development occurred frequently. It should be noted that the Expanded Programme was not the only WHO programme in the areas of human reproduction, family planning, and the health aspects of population dynamics. Other smaller programs addressed other issues such as the major factors affecting reproductive health and disease and alternative ways of providing family planning services.

In 1977, the Director-General considered that "The Expanded Programme of Research, Development and Research Training in Human Reproduction exemplifies both this evolutionary process and the Organization's ability to develop, fund, and coordinate a large worldwide research effort in response to requests from the World Health Assembly and Member States. This programme, which began in 1972, now coordinates research and training activities involving hundreds of scientists from nearly 70 countries and has become the

---

[152] HR/71.4 pt. 1, *supra* note 121, at 6.
[153] *See* HR/71.4 pt. 2, *supra* note 127, app. G at 218.
[154] *Id.* at 170.
[155] HR/71.4 add. 1, *supra* note 145, at 20-21.
[156] HR/72.5a, *supra* note 134.

model for the concept of special programs of research."[157] It was at this time that the Expanded Programme changed its name to the Special Programme for Research, Development and Training in Human Reproduction. The concept of "special research and training programmes" was originally developed to address health problems in developing countries while recognizing the lack of support for research and training in this area.[158] Thus, the coordination of research programs was considered to be the cornerstone of WHO's research activity (this implies full responsibility for the organization, implementation, funding, and communication of ongoing research).[159] These elements were approved by resolution WHA30.40 of 1977.[160] The Health Assembly also confirmed the will of the General Assembly to strengthen the mechanisms for the development and coordination of research, in particular through the support of scientific *Task forces* and by increasing the number of collaborating centers in the world. Finally, it requested the Director-General "to further elaborate the WHO long-term programme in the field of development and coordination of biomedical and health services research."

Advisory Group

To administer the program, it was proposed in 1971 "to establish a scientific Advisory Group of up to 12 high level consultants to advise WHO on its Expanded Programme in Human Reproduction."[161] Another WHO document refers to 12-15 members of eminent scientists

---

[157] World Health Organization [WHO], A30/9, *Development and Coordination of Biomedical and Health Services Research: Report by the Director-General*, at 4 (May 1977), https://apps.
who.int/iris/handle/10665/149098?search-result=true&query=A30%2F9&scope=&rpp=10&sort_by=score&order=desc [hereinafter A30/9].
[158] *Id.* at 7.
[159] *Id.* at 9-10.
[160] World Health Organization [WHO], Res. WHA30.40, *On Development and Coordination of Biomedical and Health Services Research*, (May 18, 1977), *in* 30th World Health Assembly, Geneva, 2-19 May 1977, Part I: Resolutions and Decisions, at 22-23 (1977), https://apps.who.int/iris/handle/10665/93203?search-result=true&query=WHA30.40&scope=&rpp=10&sort_by=score&order=desc.
[161] HR/71.4 pt. 1, *supra* note 121, at 7.

to advise WHO on research policy, strategies, priorities and resource allocation.[162] Annex G of the WHO report of May 1971 specifies the function and responsibilities of the *Advisory Group.*[163] Thus, it is stated that its members are appointed by the Director-General from among selected scientists in various fields related to human reproduction, appointed for a period of three years renewable once or more (with a two-year period before the third term). The terms were to be staggered so that every year one-third of the members would be renewed. One of the members was to be designated as chair by the Director-General. It was also foreseen that the role of secretary of the *Advisory Group* would be assumed by a WHO staff member. Two meetings of the *Advisory Group* were to be held each year.

The Programme was thus implemented by the *Advisory Group,* which met for the first time in November 1971. In January 1972, document HR/71.9 specified the strategy and implementation of the Programme recommended by the *Advisory Group* at this first meeting. The purpose of the meeting was to "recommend research strategy, plans and policy for the Expanded Programme, advise on the allocation of resources and report on the progress of research and development on fertility regulation."[164]Their recommendations were made by consensus or by secret ballot in case of disagreement. The review of the technical details of specific projects, however, was delegated to the *Review Group.*[165] As needed, the Advisory Group could also be assisted in its work by additional consultants, subcommittees, and study groups.[166] The group's recommendations on Programme direction, whether strategic or resource-related, were to be submitted to the Director-General. Recommendations on specific projects and proposals within the

[162] HR/71.4 add. 1, *supra* note 145, at 4.
[163] HR/71.4 pt. 2, *supra* note 127, at app. G at 218, https://apps.who.int/iris/bitstream/handle/10665/361192/HR-71.4-Pt2-eng.pdf?sequence=2&isAllowed=y.
[164] HR/72.5a, *supra* note 134, at 32.
[165] *Id.* at 32.
[166] HR/71.4 pt. 2, *supra* note 127, app. G.

approved Programme categories were to be submitted to the Assistant Director-General for approval and implementation.[167]

It is possible to determine that 10 years later, in 1980, the Advisory Group was still exercising its role in evaluating the work of the Program.[168] The Advisory Group has also always had the role of setting research priorities, taking into account a variety of influences: recommendations from the World Health Assembly and Regional Committees, requests from Member States, guidance from the *Advisory Committee on Medical Research* (ACMR), opinions from governments providing financial support to the Program, and the advice of scientific experts who participate in the Program's planning and review committees.[169]

Co-sponsorship and the changing structure of the Programme from 1986 onward

In 1986, a document[170] referred to a "Policy and Coordination Advisory Committee (PCAC)." This Committee, which appears to be an evolution of the Advisory Group, "acts as an advisory body to the Director-General of WHO, making recommendations on matters related to the policies, strategies, financing, overall organization, management and impact of the WHO Special Programme of Research, Development and Research Training in Human Reproduction (HRP)." The Committee could not have more than thirty members who had to come from different parts of the world. These members fell into four categories. First, the twelve countries that had been the largest financial contributors to the Programme the previous year. Second, twelve member states elected by the WHO regional committees for a three-year

---

[167] *Id.*

[168] A33/9, *supra* note 139, at 21 § 4.

[169] *Id.* at § 6.

[170] WHO Reg'l Comm. E. Mediterranean, EM/RC33/13, *Nomination of a member state to the Policy and Coordination advisory committee (PCAC) of the Special Programme of Research, Development, and Research Training in Human Reproduction (HRP)*, 33d Sess., (July 1986), https://apps.who.int/iris/bitstream/handle/10665/120636/em_rc33_13_en.pdf?sequence=1&isAllowed=y.

term, with one-third rotating each year. Third, up to three members elected by the ACCP for a one-year term, selected from other interested countries and nongovernmental organizations (governments, agencies, foundations, and other organizations could declare their candidacy sixty days before the ACCP meeting at which time the selection would be made). And fourth, the permanent members UNFPA, the World Bank and IPPF, which, "by their policies and financial/operational contributions, have shown an interest in the field of population/Family planning."[171]

There is no record of ACCP meeting reports outside of 1986[172] and 1987.[173] In the 1987 meeting, the Director-General, when questioned by the Chair of the ACCP, referred to the last meeting of that Committee six months earlier. A proposal for UNDP/UNFPA/WHO/World Bank co-sponsorship of the program, with WHO acting as executing agency, was on the agenda at the time: "PCAC would, as a result of this co-sponsorship, no longer act in an advisory capacity but would assume the responsibility of a governing body and would thus change its title to Policy and Coordination Committee (PCC)."[174] The purpose of this co-sponsorship was to hopefully obtain more consistent and stable funding and better access to national government structures. Dr. Barzelatto, HRP's director at the time, also told us that the Programme was giving "technical advice to both UNFPA and IPPF, two agencies which were heavily involved in global distribution of contraceptive methods."[175] The document also notes that the ACCP approved the STAG reports and considered those of the Special Programme Director.

---

[171] *Id.* at 2.

[172] World Health Organization [WHO], Meeting Report, *Special Programme of Research, Development and Research Training in Human Reproduction. Policy and Coordination Advisory Committee*, (1986), https://apps.who.int/iris/handle/10665/62386.

[173] World Health Organization, HRP/PCAC(4)/1987, *WHO Special Programme of Research, Development and Research Training in Human Reproduction : meeting of the Policy and Coordination Advisory Committee (PCAC)*, (May 1987), https://apps.who.int/iris/bitstream/handle/10665/61498/HRP_PCAC%284%29_1987.pdf?sequence=1&isAllowed=y.

[174] *Id.* at 4.

[175] *Id.* at 5.

On a practical level, it was proposed that a *Standing committee*, whose members would be representatives of the cosponsoring agencies, would meet three times a year to review the status of the Special Programme and make recommendations to the PCC. This co-sponsorship was to take effect from 1988, after the governing bodies of the sponsoring institutions had examined a "Memorandum on the administrative structure of the Special Programme of research, development and research training in human reproduction."[176] This memorandum began by recalling the purpose of the Special Programme and its basic structure. This document also makes it possible to understand that the "cooperating Parties" to the Programme are the governments and NGOs that make contributions to the Programme or offer technical or scientific support.[177] It is also the case with governments that "address the needs for fertility regulation and family planning for their populations." The funds allocated to the Special Programme were then managed by the WHO Voluntary Fund for Health Promotion.[178] The Programme was directed by several bodies, including the *Policy and Coordination Committee* (PCC).[179]

Executing Agency: WHO

WHO is the Executing agency of the Programme. In this capacity, it appoints the Director of the Special Programme and appoints or assigns all other staff of the Programme after consultation with the *Standing Committee.* The Director of the Special Programme works under the responsibility of the Assistant Director-General of WHO and with the resources of WHO. He is responsible for the overall development and implementation of the Special Programme at the scientific and technical level, including action plans and budget.[180]

---

[176] World Health Organization [WHO], EB81/22, *Recent Developments in Human Reproduction Research, Progress Report by the Director-General,* at 12 (Oct. 16, 1987), https://apps.who.int/iris/handle/10665/162389 [hereinafter EB81/22].
[177] *Id.* at § 1.2.
[178] *Id.* at § 1.5.
[179] *Id.* at §2.
[180] *Id.*

Policy and Coordination Committee - PCC

The PCC consists of 32 members selected from the "cooperating parties." Eleven of these members are representatives of the governments of the major contributing states, fourteen are representatives of States elected by the WHO regional committees for a three-year term, and two are elected by the PCC for a three-year term and selected from the other cooperating parties. Finally, the co-sponsors of the Special Programme and the *International Planned Parenthood Federation* (IPPF) are permanent members of the PCC. Subject to WHO approval and after consultation with the *Standing Committee,* other "cooperating parties" may also be observers, at their own expense. The purpose of the *Policy and Coordination Committee* is to "coordinat[e] the interests and responsibilities of the parties cooperating in the Special Programme." It is responsible for reviewing and deciding on the preparation and implementation of the Special Programme. The *Policy and Coordination Committee* thus examines the reports and recommendations submitted to it by the *Standing Committee,* by the executing agency (WHO) and by the *Scientific and Technical Advisory Group* (STAG), whose members it approves. These reports and recommendations include the action plan, budget, funding, and status updates on the program's progress in achieving its objectives.[181] The PCC meets at least once a year and secretarial services are provided by WHO. Each year, it also elects from among its' members a chairperson who convenes and chairs the meetings, a vice-chairperson, and a rapporteur. The latter is responsible for preparing a meeting report with the assistance of the secretariat, which is circulated as soon as possible after the end of the session and submitted to the participants for approval. During its sessions, the PCC strictly applies the rules of procedure of the World Health Assembly.[182]

---

[181] *Id.* at 13.

[182] *Id.* at 14.

Standing committee

The *Standing Committee* is composed of representatives of the Cosponsoring organizations. It meets twice a year and is responsible for reviewing the action plans and budget of the Special Programme as prepared by WHO and reviewed by the STAG. Its role also includes making proposals to the PCC for funding of the Programme and preparing an annual report on its own activities for the PCC. WHO is responsible for supporting the work of the *Standing Committee.*[183]

Scientific and Technical Advisory Group (STAG)

The *Scientific and Technical Advisory Group* (STAG) consists of 10-15 members who represent in their individual capacities the various elements of the broad spectrum of biomedical disciplines. They are selected by WHO, in consultation with the *Standing Committee,* and with the approval of the PCC, on the basis of their scientific and technical expertise. They are appointed for a period of three years, renewable once. The STAG's mandate includes a scientific and technical review of the content, size and scope of the Special Program, including appropriate research areas and approaches. It also reviews the action plans and budget provided by WHO and makes recommendations on the priorities of the Special Programme or on the need to discontinue a *Task Force.* STAG also provides the PCC and the *Standing Committee* with an independent and continuous evaluation of the scientific and technical aspects of all the activities of the Special Program. In its areas of responsibility, it can propose to them and to WHO any document and recommendation of a technical nature that it deems useful. The STAG meets at least once a year. WHO provides secretariat services for the STAG and also offers ongoing scientific, technical, and administrative support. Each year, the STAG issues a report based on a comprehensive review of all scientific and technical aspects of the Special Programme. Its conclusions and recommendations are thus communicated to the WHO and the *Standing Committee.* The *Standing*

---

[183] *Id.* at 14-15.

Committee then forwards the report to the PCC with its comments and those of WHO. The Chairman of STAG (or in his absence a member of STAG) attends all sessions of the *Policy and Coordination Committee* (PCC).[184]

In a 1990 HRP report, it is stated with respect to STAG that its members serve in their personal capacity and represent a wide range of disciplines. Their independence is guaranteed by the fact that they cannot serve on other program committees and cannot be principal investigators in studies undertaken by the program. They are also not eligible to receive awards from the Programme.[185] In 1999, the STAG, in addition to providing overall strategic technical advice on the work of the HRP, also began to assume this role for the entire RHR department.[186]

Programme evaluation mechanisms

In 1972, a *Review Group* was created. It was a multidisciplinary group of scientists created to oversee the procedures and mechanisms for the technical and ethical evaluation of projects.[187] This group was responsible for evaluating the qualifications and budget of the *Clinical Research Centres*. Their opinions were submitted to the *Advisory Group* which was then able to recommend them to the WHO.[188] The *Review Group* was composed of scientists who provided scientific and technical assessment of the *Task Forces* projects, the clinical trials proposed by WHO, and the proposals for the designation and renewal of *Clinical Research Centres*. The membership of the group varied according to the scientific nature of the projects to be evaluated. However, continuity

---

[184] *Id.* at 14-16.

[185] World Health Organization [WHO], *Research in Human Reproduction, Biennial Report 1988-1989*, at 9 (1990), https://apps.who.int/iris/handle/10665/38601 [hereinafter *Biennial Report 1988-1989*].

[186] World Health Organization [WHO], *Biennial Report of HRP 2008-2009*, (2010) https://apps.who.int/iris/handle/10665/70346 [hereinafter *HRP 2008-2009*].

[187] HR/72.5a, *supra* note 134, at 7.

[188] *Id.* at 25.

was ensured by two co-chairs and a small group of regular members.[189] The *Advisory Group* was also asked to recommend a mechanism to objectively evaluate the scientific merits of research proposals submitted to the program. One option proposed was the creation of *Study panels* composed of specialists in their field. An appropriate expert from the *Advisory Group* would then chair each group. The meetings of the *Study panels*, if established, should precede those of the *Advisory Group*.[190]

In 1987, it can be seen that this internal evaluation mechanism of the Special Programme had been consolidated and structured. It was conducted in two stages for each project and for the entire *Task Forces* program. The first step was a peer review of scientific experts conducting an evaluation, and the second step was a review by the independent group: the Programme *Review Group*, composed of scientific experts. They ensured that each project had scientific merit, was relevant to the program's objectives, and met satisfactory ethical standards. After that, when the research protocols were implemented, the research projects were then regularly evaluated by the STAG. In addition, each research program underwent a thorough evaluation every four years. There was also a mechanism for external evaluation of program activities. It was conducted under the auspices of the PCAC.[191] In 1987, the Director-General also insisted on the ethical aspect of the Special Programme, which he considered fundamental. The projects were thus all examined by the *Steering Committee* of each Task Force concerned, by the *Toxicology Panel* of the Special Programme, by the *Review Group* and by the WHO *Ethics Committee* (Secretariat Committee on Research Involving Human Subjects - SCRIHS).[192] The *Steering Committee* were composed of scientists with a particular expertise in the research field of the *Task Forces* whose work it guided.

[189] *Id.* at 32.
[190] HR/71.4 pt. 2, *supra* note 127, app. G.
[191] EB81/22, *supra* note 176, at 10-11.
[192] *Id.* at 9.

The budget of these task forces was fixed by the PCC on the advice of the STAG.[193]

In 1990, a *Scientific and Ethical Review Group*[194] also ensured the highest standards in the work of the program. This WHO body of independent scientists was responsible for approving projects before they could be funded. The Programme's *Toxicology Panel* also had to approve studies involving the use of new drugs or a new use of an existing drug.[195] Internal and external evaluation mechanisms were also always in place. The internal mechanisms included regular evaluations of activities by the scientific committees and more in-depth reviews by the STAG. The WHO Director-General regularly submitted a report on the activities of the Program to the WHO Executive Board and the World Health Assembly. In addition to these internal mechanisms, external evaluations of the program were also conducted by independent experts.[196]

The validation by the States of the organization and the co-sponsorship

In 1988, the WHO Executive Board noted with satisfaction the progress made by the Special Programme,[197] and the World Health Assembly endorsed these general directions,[198] especially the evaluation and

---

[193] *Biennial Report 1988-1989, supra* note 185, at 10.

[194] In 2023 - *Research ethic review committee*: WHO body, of all research projects involving human beings, receiving financial and/or technical support from WHO. It is not a committee of the HRP or SRH.

[195] *Biennial Report 1988-1989, supra* note 185, at 11.

[196] *Id.* at 13-14.

[197] WHO Executive Board Res. EB81.R6, *On Special Programme of Research, Development and Research Training in Human Reproduction,* (January 15, 1988), *in* 81st session, Geneva, 11-20 January 1988, Resolutions and Decisions, at 3-4 (1988), https://apps.who.int/iris/handle/10665/162488?search-result=true&query=EB81.R6&scope=&rpp=10&sort_by=score&order=desc.

[198] World Health Organization [WHO], Res. WHA41.9, *On Special Programme of Research, Development and Research Training in Human Reproduction*, (May 11, 1988), *in* 41st World Health Assembly, Geneva, 2-13 May 1988, Resolutions and Decisions, at 6-7 (1988), https://apps.who.int/iris/handle/10665/164346?search-result=true&query=WHA41.9&scope=&rpp=10&sort_by=score&order=desc.

development of fertility regulation techniques, the strengthening of national research in developing countries, the promotion of scientific and technical cooperation, and the coordination of research. It also reaffirmed the "close relationship between family planning, health and development, and the necessity to integrate family planning activities with those of maternal and child health." It likewise emphasized the importance of the rapid application of the results of the Programme's research in the countries' national health programs. Finally, the Health Assembly approved "the co-sponsorship of the Programme by the World Bank, the United Nations Development Programme and the United Nations Population Fund." It also urged Member States to increase their financial contributions to the Programme. In 1988, after these validations, the HRP issued its memorandum on the administrative structure of the Special Programme for Research, Development and Training in Human Reproduction.[199]

The organization of the Programme from 1998 onwards

The structure of the Programme within WHO

In 1998, the HRP merged with the WHO *Division of Technical Support for Reproductive Health* (RHT) (established in 1972). This merger created the *Department of Reproductive Health and Research* (RHR). The objective of this merger was to integrate the activities related to sexual and reproductive health research and program development within WHO into a single department.[200] The RHR Department housed and managed two programs: the HRP with its own governance structure and funding mechanism through the *HRP Trust Fund,* and the *Programme Development in Reproductive Health* (PDRH).[201] The role of the PDRH was to facilitate the implementation of the HRP research results in the

---

[199] World Health Organization [WHO], HRP/1988/1, *Memorandum on the Administrative Structure of the Special Programme of Research, Development and Research Training in Human Reproduction,* (1988), https://www.who.int/docs/default-source/hrp/hrp-admin-structure.pdf?sfvrsn=c01d0a2d_2.

[200] *Biennial Report 2006-2007, supra* note 10.

[201] *HRP 2013-2017, supra* note 4, at 2-3.

different countries.[202] This takes the form of technical advice to global partners and Member States through WHO regional and country offices.[203] The co-management of the HRP with the PDRH program within the RHR department, however, was considered complex. Financial management, on the other hand, was well separated. The HRP also collaborated extensively with other WHO departments.[204]

A 2019 report[205] outlines that now the Director and all HRP staff are appointed by WHO and work under the overall management authority of the Assistant Director-General of the *Cluster for Family, Women, Children and Adolescents* (FWC). The HRP is thus a programme entirely under the management of WHO, but not under the governance of the World Health Assembly as it has its own governing body, the PCC. As of January 2018, there were 46 people in the *Department of Reproductive Health and Research* (RHR) working under the HRP umbrella and 19 under the PDRH. All were employed by WHO, but their personal expenses were covered either by the HRP Trust Fund (for those labeled HRP) or by the Voluntary Fund of the WHO budget (for those labeled PDRH), with almost all provided funds provided as specified on a project basis. The RHR department had three teams at that time. The first one on Human Reproduction (HRX) working on contraception, genital infections, cancer, and infertility. The second on Maternal and Perinatal Health and Preventing Unsafe Abortion (MPA). And the third on Adolescents and at-Risk Populations (AGH).[206]

In 2019, as part of a WHO reform, the RHR was placed under the responsibility of the WHO Division of *UHC/Life Course* and became the *Department of Sexual and Reproductive Health and Research* (SRH) in 2019.[207] The HRP, while remaining within the SRH department, has also

---

[202] *External Evaluation 2008-2012, supra* note 1, at 1.
[203] *HRP 2013-2017, supra* note 4, at 4.
[204] *Id.* at VII.
[205] *HRP 2013-2017, supra* note 4.
[206] *Id.* at 3-5.
[207] WHO Reg'l Office Se. Asia, *HRP: Policy and Coordination Committee (PCC): Report on Attendance at PCC in 2020 Asia,* (2020), https://apps.who.int/iris/handle/10665/333620.

joined other WHO special research programs to become part of the WHO *Science Division* in order to participate more actively in setting the research agenda and producing normative guidelines on research methodologies.[208]

The organization of the Programme

In 2007, the PCC was still exercising its role and the *Standing Committee* (co-sponsors) met three times a year to guide the work of the HRP and set priorities. The HRP also had other oversight committees, including the STAG and the *Gender Advisory Panel* (GAP). The HRP also conducted its own financial oversight by reporting on the financial status of the Programme to the PCC. The Programme then functioned as a trust fund within the RHR, providing support to the department's research portfolio.[209]

The *Gender Advisory Panel* (GAP) was created in 1995[210] and renamed the *Gender and Rights Advisory Panel* in 2007 without changing the acronym GAP. In 2012, the panel had eight members. According to another document,[211] it was established by the PCC in 1996. In 2014, the GAP's mandate was formalized as an advisory body to the RHR department (rather than to HRP) on gender and rights issues.[212] His reports were presented at the STAG and PCC meetings. In turn, the *Research Project Review Panel* (RP2) was responsible for reviewing each HRP research project by providing scientific, financial, technical, and ethical review. No research proposal could be funded by the HRP without the final approval of the RP2.[213] The RP2 was formed in 2008 from the merger of five pre-existing specialist panels with the *Scientific and Ethics Review Group*. This has led to a simplified and faster but equally rigorous review process. It appears, however, that despite this

[208] *HRP Annual Report 2020, supra* note 8, at 4.
[209] *Biennial Report 2006-2007, supra* note 10, at 43.
[210] *External Evaluation 2008-2012, supra* note 1, at 21.
[211] *HRP 2013-2017, supra* note 4, at 4.
[212] *Id.* at 46.
[213] *External Evaluation 2008-2012, supra* note 1, at 19.

process, all HRP research projects must also be submitted to and approved by the WHO *Research Ethics Review Committee* (ERC). Between 2010 and 2012, the Program had to pay nearly $250,000 for this additional review process, which was considered redundant.[214] In 2010, at the global regional level, *Regional Advisory Panels* (RAP) also performed a monitoring and evaluation role and set the research strategy at an annual meeting. From an ethical point of view, the *Research Project Review Panel* (RP2) also reviewed each project involving human or animal subjects. In a complementary way, the *Toxicology Panel* evaluated the active ingredients and devices tested by the HRP (pharmacokinetics, carcinogenicity, mutagenicity...).[215]

The PCC met annually for two days to review the annual program and performance reports of the HRP, the reports of the Standing Committee, STAG, and GAP (since 1996), and the annual financial reports. After consulting the reports and recommendations provided by WHO, the *Standing Committee*, STAG, and GAP, it would then present several thematic issues for discussion before presenting the work program and budget for the next biennium (every other meeting) and invite financial donors to commit funds for the following year. In this way, the PCC was able to make up to 50 recommendations or decisions at each meeting.[216] It appears, however, that over time the *Standing Committee* has reduced its role in the governance of the program by no longer making substantive recommendations but rather formulating its decisions in the form of acknowledgements.[217]

Thus, before each meeting, the HRP Director and the STAG and GAP Chairs informed the PCC of the progress of their work.[218] The STAG and GAP also provided advice and guidance on the work of the

---

[214] *Id.* at 22.

[215] *HRP 2008-2009, supra* note 186, at 4.

[216] *HRP 2013-2017, supra* note 4, at 44.

[217] *Id.* at 46.

[218] World Health Organization [WHO], *HRP at 40: What They Say: a History of Scientific Achievement to Advance Sexual and Reproductive Health*, at 1 (2012), https://apps.who.int /iris/handle/10665/70911 [hereinafter *HRP at 40*].

HRP/RHR, presenting their assessments annually to help develop plans for the following year. RP2 and the *Toxicology Panel* also provided expertise. Finally, the GAP ensured that gender equity and equality considerations and reproductive rights were taken into account in the department's work. It also provided advice on gender and human rights research related to sexual and reproductive health.[219] STAG and GAP meet annually in back-to-back meetings. It also appears that in 2014, an *HRP Alliance Steering Committee* was formed. The Committee incorporates the former *Regional Advisory Panels* (RAP) of the HRP. It began reporting to the CCP in 2015.[220] It appears that the costs of STAG and GAP that were to be borne by PDRH and HRP have been entirely borne by HRP since 2009.[221] Through their meetings, PCC members contributed to the global research agenda on sexual and reproductive health.

The evolution of co-sponsorship and the revision of the 2012 Memorandum

A document to evaluate the organization of the Programme was published in 2008.[222] This year, the HRP considered finding new co-sponsors. UNICEF was one of the candidates considered among others because of its links with the activities of the HRP (work for the spacing of the pregnancies in particular).[223] In December 2012, UNICEF became a new co-sponsor of the HRP and UNAIDS became a new permanent member of the PCC, joining IPPF in this capacity. That same year, the HRP's Memorandum of Administrative Structure was revised accordingly.[224] Co-sponsorship of the HRP is governed by this

---

[219] *Id.* at 4-5.
[220] *HRP 2013-2017, supra* note 4, at 42.
[221] *External Evaluation 2008-2012, supra* note 1, at 20-21.
[222] World Health Organization [WHO], *External Evaluation 2003-2007: Monitoring Governance, Management, Administration and Efficiency: a Case Study,* (2008), https://apps.who.int/iris/handle/10665/69895.
[223] *Id.* at 7.
[224] World Health Organization [WHO], HRP/1988/1, *Memorandum on the Administrative Structure of the Special Programme of Research, Development and Research Training in*

Memorandum which does not imply a legally binding relationship but is an expression of commitment.[225] GAP is not mentioned in the Memorandum.

The restructuring of the HRP in 2020

Since January 2020, HRP has been restructured into eight units, each responsible for a technical area.[226] First, the HRP Secretariat (SRT) "is responsible for HRP governing and advisory bodies, strategic and operational planning, finance and administration, communications, global advocacy, fundraising and partner engagement." Then the *Research Leadership and Capacity Strengthening* (RLC) unit "coordinates HRP's work on research agenda setting, research methodology development, research capacity strengthening, scientific and ethical review processes, study design, statistical and data management and analysis support, and research partner engagement." Then, the *Contraception and Fertility Care* (CFC) unit "develops guidelines and recommendations; coordinates research, evidence synthesis, development and innovation; provides specialized technical support; and disseminates information on evidence-based practices in contraception and fertility care, including infertility management and treatment of associated conditions." Finally, five other units work on research and development, innovation, evidence synthesis, development of guidelines and recommendations, provision of expert technical support, and dissemination of information on evidence-based practices, each in their thematic area:

- The *Addressing Needs of Vulnerable Populations* (AVP) unit which "seeks to overcome discrimination and inequalities in sexual and reproductive health." It works "on issues such as adolescence, gender-based violence, traditional and harmful

Human Reproduction (HRP), (rev. 2012), https://cdn.who.int/media/docs/default-source/hrp/hrp-mou-admin-structure-rev-2012.pdf?sfvrsn=de99f821_2.

[225] *External Evaluation 2008-2012, supra* note 1, at 18.

[226] *HRP Annual Report 2020, supra* note 8, at 4-5.

practices; health emergencies and migration; disability; and sexual orientation and gender identity".

- The *Maternal and Perinatal Health* (MPH) unit.
- The *Prevention of Unsafe Abortion* (PUA) unit which works "on evidence-based practices on prevention of unsafe abortion, including safe abortion services and post-abortion care."
- The *Sexual and Reproductive Health Integration into Health Systems* (SHS) unit which is working towards the achievement of Universal health coverage (UHC).
- The *Sexual Health and Reproductive Cancers* (SRC) unit which works on sexually transmitted infections, reproductive cancers, and sexual well-being and pleasure.

The financing

The beginnings of the Programme

After the study report was circulated to interested organizations in 1970, the strategy was approved and contributions of over $4.5 million were pledged to the WHO Voluntary Fund for Health Promotion for the first year of the programme.[227] In 1971, WHO planned[228] to spend $6.7 million between 1971 and 1972, $9.4 million between 1972 and 1973, and $12.5 to $22.2 million between 1973 and 1976, to implement the orientations decided at the founding of the Programme and to finance WHO's technical support.[229] The Director-General anticipated that the new positions in the WHO Expanded Programme on Human Reproduction Research would be "financed not only from the regular budget but also from sources such as the United Nations Fund for Population Activities [UNFPA], [and] voluntary contributions both governmental and otherwise" paid directly to the Programme.[230] The

---

[227] *HR/71.9*, *supra* note 120.

[228] HR/71.4 pt. 1, *supra* note 121.

[229] *See also* HR/71.4 pt. 2, *supra* note 127, app. F at 8.

[230] World Health Organization [WHO], EB49/15, *Permanent Addition to the Headquarters Accommodation, Report by the Director-General,* at 1 (Nov. 26, 1971), https://apps.who.int/iris/handle/10665/145608?search-result=true&query=EB49%2F15&scope=&rpp=10&sort_by=score&order=desc.

WHO provided for this to be funded by contributions to the WHO Special Account for Medical Research[231] and administered in accordance with WHO's financial regulations. The implementation of the Programme shall commence when funds become available with the objective of being operational within twelve months.[232] WHO hoped[233] that voluntary contributions would not be earmarked by the donor for a specific project but rather for the Programme in general so that they could be allocated in accordance with the *Advisory Group*'s strategy.[234]

In his biannual budget proposal published in 1971, the Director-General of WHO takes into account the new Human Reproduction Programme.[235] The costs of the research support for different projects in the programme are defined.[236] For example, the programme received $10,000 for clinical and epidemiological studies on the health effects of abortion and it received $40,000 for preclinical, clinical and epidemiological studies on various methods of fertility regulation. The programme received an estimated total of $2,573,000 between 1971 and 1973; notably, $461,900 came from the regular budget and $2,111,100 from other sources.[237] It is also estimated that an additional $6,800 and $6,400 were allocated for a meeting on the programme and a meeting of the contributing agencies to the programme.[238]

In 1970, a single voluntary financial contribution of $50,000 was made by the Swedish International Development Authority (SIDA). In 1971, contributions amounted to US $3,151,500 and were made by three

---

[231] Account based on §10(1) of Res. WHA12.17 of 1959, https://apps.who.int/iris/bitstream/handle/10665/88804/WHA12.17_eng.pdf?sequence=1&isAllowed=y.

[232] HR/71.4 pt. 1, *supra* note 121,at 9-10.

[233] According to G. Benagiano, it was in fact a "conditio sine qua non." E-mail from G. Benagiano, Director of HRP 1993-97, to Louis-Marie Bonneau, ECLJ (Jan. 25, 2023 15:59 CEST) (on file with recipient).

[234] HR/71.4 add. 1, *supra* note 145,at 22.

[235] World Health Organization [WHO], *Proposed Programme and Budget Estimates for 1973*, at 100 (1971), https://apps.who.int/iris/handle/10665/85838.

[236] *Id.* at 505-506.

[237] *Id.* at 521-522.

[238] *Id.* at 610.

organizations. The International Development Research Centre (IDRC - Canada) contributed $51,500, the Ford Foundation contributed $100,000, and SIDA allocated $3,000,000. Finally, in 1972, four organizations also contributed $1,254,000 to the program. Broken down, $500,000 came from the Ford Foundation (and also $400,000 available in 1973), $100,000 from the IDRC with, and $454,000 from the Norwegian Agency for International Development (NORAD), and $200,000 from the Danish International Development Agency (DANIDA), (received through the United Nations Fund for Population Activities - UNFPA).[239] In 1972, the Expanded Programme had also benefited from the technical and administrative services provided by WHO.[240] Another 1972 document reported that interest in human reproductive research had resulted in voluntary contributions in the range of $4 to $5 million per year.[241] Thus, the Expanded Programme was financed in the first year (1971-1972) by voluntary contributions to the Special Account for Medical Research amounting to $4,400,000.[242]

Follow-up on the growth of the Expanded Programme

In November 1973, a projection of the work of the Expanded Programme between 1974 and 1976 was published.[243] First, the budget was estimated to grow over the years, from $2.9 million in 1972 and $6.5 million in 1973 to a projected budget of $10.5 million in 1974, $12.6 million in 1975, and $14.5 million in 1976. *Task forces*, then, represented

---

[239] HR/72.5a, *supra* note 134, at 34.

[240] *Id.* at 3.

[241] World Health Organization [WHO], Report A25/30, *On Headquarters Accommodation: Future Requirements, in* 25th World Health Assembly, Geneva, 9-26 May 1972, Part I: resolutions and decisions, at 3 (1972), https://apps.who.int/iris/handle/10665/145478?search-result=true&query=A25%2F30&scope=&rpp=10&sort_by=score&order=desc.

[242] World Health Organization [WHO],*The Work of WHO 1972, Annual Report of the Director-General to the World Health Assembly and to the United Nations,* 134-139 (1973), https://apps.who.int/iris/handle/10665/85854?search-result=true&query=The+work+of+WHO+1972%2C&scope=&rpp=10&sort_by=score&order=desc [hereinafter *Work of WHO 1972*].

[243] World Health Organization [WHO], HR/73.5c, *Expanded Programme of Research, Development and Research Training in Human Reproduction: projections 1974-1976, November 1973*, (1973),
https://apps.who.int/iris/handle/10665/361197.

three-fifths of the budget. They were, in fact, the most complex part of the Expanded Programme because of the large number of research projects involving frequent decision making.[244] For example, the budget for the *Task Force* on the Acceptability of Birth Control Methods was projected to increase from $156,000 in 1973 to $620,000 in 1976; and the budget for the *Task Force* on Immunology was projected to increase from $288,000 to $1.2 million for the same dates. The document also details the projected costs and budgets for each aspect of the *Task forces'* work.

It was also anticipated that support for research training would grow as a result of the recruitment of full-time staff members for this purpose. In general, the budget projections reflected the Expanded Programme's desire for growth.

In 1973, the expansion of the Expanded Programme was accompanied by the creation of additional posts and costs for WHO. To fund the program, several agencies offered grants, such as, the Canadian ($1,000,000), Danish ($364,000), and Norwegian ($666,000) International Development Agencies; the Swedish International Development Authority (SIDA) ($4,000,000); and the Ford Foundation ($200,000). This amounted to $6,230,000 in that year.[245]

The will to sustain the resources of the Expanded Programme

In 1977, the Director-General noted that the Programme represented the most important research activity of WHO while being almost exclusively financed by voluntary funds.[246] In that same year, the Programme was mainly financed by contributions to the Voluntary Fund for Health Promotion from Canada, Denmark, Finland, India,

---

[244] *Id.* at 3-4.
[245] World Health Organization [WHO], *Expanded Programme of Research, Development and Research Training in Human Reproduction: Second Annual Report, November 1973 –* HR/73.5a (1973), https://apps.who.int/iris/handle/10665/361196 [hereinafter *HR/73.5a*].
[246] A30/9, *supra* note 157, at 20.

Mexico, Norway and the United Kingdom.[247] In 1980, however, the Programme felt that it lacked resources despite the new contributions from three Member States in 1979, and the standing contributions from other Member States.[248] With the goal of achieving "health for all by the year 2000." the *Advisory Committee on Medical Research* (ACMR) recommended that "every effort be made to increase the donor base of the Special Programme of Research, Development and Research Training in Human Reproduction, in order to ensure the Programme's durability and further development."[249]

In 1980, the Special Programme was the world's largest family planning research training programme, with an expenditure of $2 million. This resulted in a doubling of research grants awarded from 1979 and the organization of research training courses. These expenditures were "largely financed by voluntary contributions." In 1980, donors included Australia, Cuba, Denmark, Finland, India, Nigeria, Norway, the Federal Republic of Germany, the United Kingdom, Sweden, Thailand, and UNFPA.[250]

In 1983, a document[251] from the Southeast Asian Consultative Committee on Medical Research related to the HRP revealed that since the beginning of the program, countries in the Southeast Asian region had received more than $13 million to support research and build

---

[247] World Health Organization [WHO], EB61/23, *Development and Coordination of Biomedical and Health Services Research: Report by the Director-General,* (Dec. 1, 1977), *in* Special Programme of Research, Development and Research Training in Human Reproduction, Annex I at 14 § 6.1 (1977), https://apps.who.int/iris/handle/10665/153639?search-result=true&query=EB61%2F23&scope=&rpp=10&sort_by=score&order=desc [hereinafter EB61/23].

[248] A33/9, *supra* note 139, at 22 § 14.

[249] *Id.* at 23.

[250] World Health Organization [WHO], A34/3, *Report of the Director-General on the work of WHO in 1980,* (Apr. 1, 1981), *in* 34th World Health Assembly Geneva, 4-22 May 1981, Resolutions and Decisions, Annex 4 § 105 (1981), https://apps.who.int/iris/handle/10665/155588?search-result=true&query=A34%2F3&scope=&rpp=10&sort_by=score&order=desc [hereinafter A34/3].

[251] WHO & S.E. Asia Advisory Comm. on Med. Rsch., SEA/ACMR/9/11, *Special Programme on Research Development and Research Training in Human Reproduction,* (Feb. 21, 1983), https://apps.who.int/iris/handle/10665/127360.

research capacity (between $1.5 and $2 million per year). It also revealed that in addition to the Programme's *Advisory Group*, the Programme's donors had made recommendations on the direction of the research.[252] These recommendations from states were in the normal course of the PCC's work.

Between 1971 and 1987, 25 contributors (including seven developing countries) had offered financial support of some $200 million.[253] These contributions increased to $19 million in 1980, declined to a minimum of $12.5 million in 1984, and then increased again to nearly $21 million in 1987.[254] In-kind grants were also provided by various institutions in the form of personnel and institutional infrastructure. The Special Programme also acted as the implementing agency for UNFPA's national projects. STAG was responsible for maintaining an appropriate balance in the allocation of resources to the various activities of the Special Programme.[255]

Between 1970 and 1999, the Programme received contributions from States, co-sponsors and private foundations amounting to nearly 447 million dollars.[256] The twenty biggest contributors to the HRP were, in order of importance, Sweden ($96,204,000), the UK ($72,478,000), UNFPA ($61,040,000), Norway ($48,733,000), Denmark ($29,515,000), the World Bank ($29,008,000), the USA ($19,471,000), Germany

---

[252] *Id.* at 4 : "As a consequence of recommendations made by the Programme's own Advisory Group, by donors to the Programme and by the Global and Regional Advisory Groups on Medical Research, greater emphasis had been placed on health service research and psychosocial research."

[253] EB81/22, *supra* note 176, at 9.

[254] *Id.* at 10 "The financial contributors during the biennium 1986-1987 were: Australia, China, Cuba, Denmark, Finland, France, Federal Republic of Germany, India, Malaysia, Mexico, Netherlands, Nigeria, Norway, Sweden, Thailand, Union of Soviet Socialist Republics (contribution in kind), United Kingdom of Great Britain and Northern Ireland, United States of America (contribution in kind), the Canadian International Development Research Centre, the Rockefeller Foundation, UNFPA, the World Bank, WHO."

[255] *Id.* at 9-11.

[256] World Health Organization [WHO], *Reproductive health research in WHO, a new beginning, HRP Financial Report 1998-1999*,at 11 (2000) https://apps.who.int/iris/handle/10665/66327 [hereinafter *Financial Report 1996-1998*]

($16,537,000), WHO (US$15,714,000), Canada ($10,376,000), Netherlands ($8,717,000), Australia ($4,109,000), Rockefeller Foundation ($3,681,000), Finland ($3,349,000), Switzerland ($3,247,000), Bill and Melinda Gates Foundation ($2,000,000), UNDP ($1,695,000) and Ford Foundation ($1,162,000). The amounts of the 50 contributors ranged from $96 million to $1,000.

Between 1988 and 1989, the Programme continued to be funded by voluntary contributions from Member States and other organizations in the amount of $43.4 million. In-kind contributions were also made mainly by collaborating research institutions in 80 countries.[257] In 2000, the programme's financial report showed that the Bill & Melinda Gates Foundation ($2,000,000), the William and Flora Hewlett Foundation ($150,000) and the MacArthur Foundation ($15,000) began contributing to the programme between 1998 and 1999.[258] There are also 12 grants awarded for specific research projects. For example, the Rockefeller Foundation provided $47,500 for joint funding of mission-oriented research in male fertility, the Ford Foundation provided $18,000 to support Indonesian participants at the International Conference on Reproductive Health in Mumbai, and the MacArthur Foundation provided $15,000 to support speakers from developing countries at the Conference in Mumbai.[259] The possibility for the Programme to accept designated contributions was conditionally accepted by the PCC at its June 1997 meeting.[260]

The financial state after 2000

On January 1, 2000, a new HRP Trust Fund was established to enable the Programme to raise funds.[261] A few years later, in 2004, the director

---

[257] World Health Organization: *Research in Human Reproduction, Biennial Report 1988-1989*, 1990, p.3 https://apps.who.int/iris/handle/10665/38601

[258] *Financial Report 1996-1998*, *supra* note 256, at 7.

[259] *Id.* at 12-13.

[260] *Id.* at 3.

[261] World Health Organization [WHO], *Unaudited interim financial report for the year 2000: Fiscal 2000-2001*, 54th World Health Assembly, at 4 (2001), https://apps.who.int/iris/handle/10665/83758.

warned, however, that the HRP's revenues were falling sharply, threatening its activities and even its existence.[262] In 2001, the PCC approved a budget of $40.3 million, but only $26.5 million was received, a shortfall of nearly $14 million. This led to the implementation of a more focused budget in 2002-2003.[263] By 2007, the department had returned to a healthy financial position and HRP's revenue for the biennium was $44.4 million: "The four largest Member-State contributors to RHR (and/or HRP) were the Netherlands, Norway, Sweden and the United Kingdom. The three largest contributions from foundation donors were from the David and Lucile Packard Foundation, the Ford Foundation, and the William and Flora Hewlett Foundation."[264] The 2008 external evaluation of the HRP[265] confirmed this financial improvement, noting that several donor countries had significantly increased their contributions. It appears, however, that the HRP had suffered a significant loss of income when WHO called on donors to shift their funding from a specific project or program, such as the HRP, to the general budget. It should also be noted that while UNDP had been actively engaged in the work of the Programme, it had not yet resumed its financial contributions.[266] The World Bank had been the most consistent and strongest financial supporter of the HRP between 2008 and 2012, providing 55% of Cosponsor income. UNFPA and WHO each provided 22%. Between 2008 and 2012, UNDP had resumed its financial contributions.[267] A 2008 document revealed that UNDP had not been active since 1996 in co-sponsorship, whether financially, in technical exchanges or in governance.[268] According to a 2012 document[269] tracking HRP's scientific accomplishments since 1972,

---

[262] *Biennial Report 2002-2003, supra* note 9, at 7-8.

[263] *Id.* at 39.

[264] *Biennial Report 2006-2007, supra* note 10, at 43.

[265] World Health Organization [WHO], *External Evaluation 2003-2007: Executive Summary*, (2008), https://apps.who.int/iris/handle/10665/69889.

[266] *Id.* at 21-22.

[267] *External Evaluation 2008-2012, supra* note 1, at 18-19.

[268] World Health Organization [WHO], *External Evaluation 2003-2007: Monitoring Governance, Management, Administration and Efficiency: a Case Study*, (2008), https://apps.who.int/iris/handle/10665/69895.

[269] *HRP at 40, supra* note 218, at 1.

more than 95% of HRP's income came from voluntary contributions. In 2011, the department received a grant from the French government to support reproductive health and family planning in French-speaking African countries.[270]

Regarding the cost of the HRP's work, a 2019 report states that the cost of developing a guideline is $110,000 and that a research project in maternal and perinatal health costs $590,000.[271] Regarding finances, they were considered sufficient between 2013 and 2017, although there was a trend toward an increase in the proportion of designated funds. Another cause for concern was the collapse of cosponsor funding, with the exception of regular contributions from WHO.[272]

---

[270] World Health Organization [WHO], *Highlights of 2011*, at 14-15 (2012), https://apps.who.int/iris/handle/10665/70928.
[271] *HRP 2013-2017*, *supra* note 4, at 64.
[272] *Id.* at VII.

Chapter 5
Integration of the Expanded Programme into the Biomedical Research Coordination Framework

The Expanded Programme for Research, Development and Training in Human Reproduction was developed with a demographic focus but fit, from a practical point of view, into the research coordination role assigned to WHO since resolution WHA2.19 of 1949.[273] Thus, resolution WHA25.60[274] of 1972 on WHO's role in the development and coordination of biomedical research, requested the Director-General to "prepare proposals for the development of long-term WHO activities in biomedical research within the framework of the programmes being carried out by the Organization". The Director-General reported on this in December 1972[275], by including human reproduction, and in particular the Expanded Programme, among the research programmes to be funded. According to various program directors, this 1972 resolution formally established the HRP.[276]

---

[273] World Health Organization [WHO], Res. WHA2.19, *On Co-ordination of Research, in* 2d World Health Assembly, Rome,13 June-2 July 1949, at 23 (1949), https://apps.who.int/iris/handle/10665/86082.

[274] World Health Organization [WHO], Res. WHA25.60, *On WHO's Role in the Development and Coordination of Biomedical Research,* 25th World Health Assembly, Geneva, 9-26 May 1972 - Part I: resolutions and decisions, at 32-33 (1972), https://apps.who.int/iris/handle/10665/91995?search-result=true&query=WHA25.60&scope=&rpp=10&sort_by=score&order=desc.

[275] World Health Organization [WHO], EB51/6, *WHO's Role in the Development and Coordination of Biomedical Research: Interim Report by the Director-General,* (Dec. 1972), https://apps.who.int/iris/bitstream/handle/10665/146302/EB51_6_eng.pdf?sequence=1&isAllowed=y.

[276] *See* Michael T Mbizvo, Catherine d'Arcangues, Paul FA Van Look, & Benagiano Giuseppe, *40 Years of Innovation in Sexual and Reproductive Health,* 380 THE LANCET 705-06 (2012); *and* World Health Organization [WHO], *Reflections on a dream job in sexual and reproductive health and rights,* (February 2022) https://www.who.int/news/item/20-02-2022-reflections-on-a-dream-job-in-sexual-and-reproductive-health-and-rights.

In May 1973, the Health Assembly, through Resolution WHA26.42[277], took note of the Director-General's 1972 report. It also asked the Director-General to continue his study and to submit a report on the subject. The Director-General published his report in December 1973 in which he noted among the priority research topics were those on human reproduction and fertility regulation.[278] It also cited the Expanded Programme as an example of methods in use to promote and assist research. The Programme's activity since December 1971 was summarized in the report,[279] which was taken into account by resolution WHA27.61 of May 1974.[280] In that resolution, the Health Assembly requested the Director-General to submit an annual progress report on WHO's research programme. A new report was published in December 1974.[281] It briefly discusses human reproduction and family planning activities, noting that they are reviewed by the *Advisory Committee on Medical Research* (ACMR).[282] This last report was in turn taken into account by resolution WHA28.70 of May 1975.[283]

---

[277] World Health Organization [WHO], Res. WHA26.42, *On WHO's Role in the Development and Coordination of Biomedical Research*, 26th World Health Assembly, Geneva, 7-23 May 1973: part I: resolutions and decisions, at 24 (1973), https://apps.who.int/iris/handle/10665/92135?search-result=true&query=WHA26.42 &scope=&rpp=10&sort_by=score&order=desc.

[278] World Health Organization [WHO], EB53/5, *WHO's Role in the Development and Coordination of Biomedical Research: Report by the Director-General*, at 3 §B.3 (Dec. 1973), https://apps.who.int/iris/handle/10665/147104.

[279] *Id.* at 32-33.

[280] WHO Res. WHA27.61, *On WHO's Role in the Development and Coordination of Biomedical Research*, 27th World Health Assembly, Geneva, 7-23 May 1974, Part I: resolutions and decisions, at 31 (1974), https://apps.who.int/iris/handle/10665/92782?search-result=true&query=WHA27.61&scope=&rpp=10&sort_by=score&order=desc.

[281] WHO, EB55/8, *WHO's Role in the Development and Coordination of Biomedical Research: Progress Report by the Director-General*, (Dec. 1974), https://apps.who.int/iris/bitstream/handle/10665/148377/EB55_8_eng.pdf?sequence=1&isAllowed=y.

[282] *Id.* at 2.

[283] WHO, Res. WHA28.70, *On WHO's role in the development and coordination of biomedical research*, *in* 28th World Health Assembly, Geneva, 13-30 May 1975, Part I: resolutions and decisions, at 39-40 (1975), https://apps.who.int/iris/handle/10665/93008.

The Director-General issued a new progress report in November 1976[284] in which he again mentioned WHO's work in human reproduction, and paid special attention to the Expanded Programme for Research, Development and Training in Human Reproduction's (HRP)*Research and Training Centres* and the organization of their work through *Task Forces*.[285] That year, the *Human Reproduction Unit* still existed with Giuseppe Benagiano working there as a scientist.[286] The new HRP did not make it disappear.

In 1987, the Executive Director spoke about the HRP. According to him, the HRP was a global program of international technical cooperation that promoted and supported research on various aspects of human reproduction, ranging from biomedical research to research on behavioral and social factors in the development of family planning methods. The goal was to discover and develop safe and effective methods to regulate fertility by removing barriers to this goal. To this end, national research capacity building was promoted alongside collaboration and coordination with other programs. This involved training researchers and providing technical and financial support for their research, particularly in developing countries. More concretely, the research activities of the Programme were carried out through a network of *Task Forces* supported by a worldwide collaboration of research centers. This had allowed the development of new contraceptive products and devices. The Director-General also recalled that the Programme was mainly financed by extra-budgetary resources, which amounted to approximately $21 million in 1987.[287]

---

[284] WHO, EB59/16, *Development and coordination of Biomedical and Health Services Research: Interim Report*, (Nov. 1976), https://apps.who.int/iris/handle/10665/153242.
[285] *Id.* at 4.
[286] GIUSEPPE BENAGIANO: Scientist in the Human Reproduction Unit of the World Health Organization (1973-1976). CURRICULUM VITAE OF GUISEPPE BENAGIANO, https://www.gfmer.ch/International_activities_En/PDF/Benagiano_CV_english.pdf.
[287] EB81/22, *supra* note 176.

Biomedical research on fertility regulation conducted by the Programme

In October 1972, the original sponsoring organizations and nine other interested institutions met in Geneva to review the progress of the Expanded Programme and discuss future funding that guided the programme. A report by the Director-General on WHO's work that year specified the three major lines of research chosen for fertility regulation. First, basic and applied research on new and improved methods of fertility regulation (e.g., medicated hormone-releasing intrauterine devices, new chemical and surgical methods of sterilization, research on prostaglandins and related substances). Second, research on the reproductive mechanisms that are most suitable for regulation (regulation of ovum migration, emergency contraception, regulation of implantation, including immunological methods, regulation of sperm migration and survival in the female body, and determination of the time of ovulation). Third, research to obtain the necessary basis evaluating existing methods of regulation: studies of the characteristics of different methods of fertility regulation that affect their acceptance in different socio-cultural settings, development of better pharmacological models for the screening of potential fertility regulation agents, assessment of the sequelae of vasal occlusion, study of the sequelae of abortion, research on the health hazards of repeated abortions, and research on the possible combination of abortion with a sterilization process.[288]

The research projects of the *Task Forces* included several studies on topics like the action of prostaglandins in the regulation of fertility, methods of regulating egg transport and implantation, methods of

---

[288] *Work of WHO 1972*, *supra* note 242.

regulating sperm maturation and survival, and the acceptability profiles of fertility regulation methods.[289]

The second annual report of the WHO Expanded Programme published in 1973[290] confirms that it was the *Task Forces* created in 1972 that spearheaded the development of the research activities of the Programme. That year, more than 250 scientists from 27 countries were involved. Their work was scheduled to take varying lengths of time, with some research expected to yield results in five to fifteen years, and other areas of research, such as the development of contraceptive vaccines, that the WHO was aware would take longer,.[291] This growing activity led to an increase in the number of clinical trials that were conducted in the network of *Clinical Research Centres* of the WHO Expanded Programme. The four institutions designated in 1972 as WHO *Research and Training Centres* on human reproduction also played an important role in this general research work in collaboration with the *Clinical Research Centres* and *Task Forces*. The *Advisory Group* also continued to guide the work of the programme with two meetings in 1973. The *Review Group* also continued to evaluate the scientific merit and ethical aspects of the various research projects.

The Special Programme thus covered a multitude of areas of human reproduction (biomedical, epidemiological and operational aspects of family planning, infertility, pregnancy...) making it one of the largest research programmes of the Organization. According to the Director-General, in a report to the World Health Assembly and the United Nations published in 1973: if human reproduction research had been a neglected field until then, the interest in family planning and the

---

[289] World Health Organization [WHO], HR/71.9, *Expanded Programme of Research, Development and Research Training in Human Reproduction: Programme Strategy and Implementation*; (1972), https://apps.who.int/iris/handle/10665/361191 [hereinafter *HR/71.9 Expanded Programme*].

[290] *HR/73.5a, supra* note 245.

[291] *Id.* at 3.

awareness of its impact on the health of the individual and the family gave it more attention.[292]

In 1988-1989, eight *Task forces* were still at work. Their work was mainly aimed at improving the methods already in use as well as developing new ones.[293] Groups were dedicated to researching the safety and efficacy of fertility regulation methods, the behavioral and social determinants of fertility regulation, vaccines for fertility regulation, male fertility regulation methods and natural fertility regulation methods. Finally, another group was dedicated to researching the prevention and management of infertility.[294]

The origin and development of contraceptive, sterilizing and abortifacient products

The development of female contraceptives and abortion

In 1971, the Director-General reviewed research on fertility reduction methods. He noted the effectiveness of oral contraceptives and intrauterine devices on women but also that their use posed problems.[295] That year, the WHO decided that it was easier to control reproduction of women than of men, because a single intervention at a given moment can interfere with the entire reproductive process at different times: ovulation, embryonic development or sperm transport. However, considering that the timing of the intervention in relation to ovulation was absolutely critical, it was thought that the discovery of a simple technique to detect ovulation would be a major achievement.[296] This aspect was thus, from the beginning of the programme, a research axis considered important because of the very short fertilizable life of the ovum.[297] A *Task force* was then interested in simple methods of prediction and detection of ovulation in order to make more effective

[292] *Work of WHO 1972, supra* note 242.
[293] *Biennial Report 1988-1989, supra* note 185, at 4 (1990).
[294] *Id.* at 9.
[295] *Work of WHO 1971, supra* note 123, at 132 § 8.29.
[296] HR/71.4 add. 1, *supra* note 145, at 4.
[297] *HR/71.9 Expanded Programme, supra* note 289.

the methods of fertility regulation which require a precise synchronization with ovulation.[298]

In 1971, the Director-General also noted the considerable interest in the use of prostaglandins for fertility control.[299] In March 1971, a conference-workshop gathering most of the researchers working on this subject was organized in Stockholm at the WHO *Research and Training Centre* for Human Reproduction (then directed by Dr. Egon Dicsfaluzy).[300] The Director-General stated that the primary criteria for evaluating contraceptive methods should be efficacy and "the safety of the user and the well-being of any offspring that may be born should there be contraceptive failure".[301] In an effort to reduce fertility, research was also conducted on agents that interfere with embryonic development, particularly the various prostaglandins, to determine their mechanisms of action in inducing abortion. The development of other abortifacients from synthetic or natural sources was another line of research considered important.[302]

A few years later, in 1977, a review of WHO research on new or improved methods of contraception recorded, among other things, research on chemical sterilization for women, abortifacients (e.g. prostaglandins and plant products), anti-pregnancy vaccines and vaccines acting against sperm and eggs. The report stated that, although these methods were still uncertain and WHO could stop research if they were unsuccessful, birth control vaccines and fertility control substances for men were in the early stages of development.[303] The side effects of some contraceptives were also noted, such as the pill, which can cause thromboembolism. He went on to note that there are many unanswered questions about these side effects, including whether hormonal contraceptives are carcinogenic, whether intrauterine devices

---

[298] *HR/73.5a, supra* note 245, at 25.
[299] *Work of WHO 1971, supra* note 123, at 132 § 8.29.
[300] HR/71.4 pt. 2, *supra* note 127, at 170.
[301] *Work of WHO 1971, supra* note 123, at 135 § 8.46.
[302] HR/71.4 add. 1, *supra* note 145.
[303] EB61/23, *supra* note 247, at 7-15.

can lead to sterility, whether abortion endangers subsequent pregnancies, and to what extent sterilization, of men or women, can lead to psychological disorders.[304] The report noted that there is no such thing as an "ideal contraceptive" because each person has his or her own preferences, so the idea was to offer a range of different methods.[305] For this reason, it called for continued research in the field of human reproduction to evaluate the safety, efficacy and acceptability of the methods used to improve contraceptives or create new ones.[306]

By 1980, several components had been developed, such as a fertility timing kit, chemical methods of female sterilization, and the use of prostaglandins for abortions. The programme also continued to conduct psycho-social research, including research on the influence of illegal abortion on health. Other research focused on the factors that determine the choice and continued use of fertility regulation methods, male and female sterilization performed by non-physicians, beliefs, and the integration of family planning with other health activities.[307] This year, the Director-General also announced that guidelines had been established "on the relative safety and efficacy of different oral contraceptives, intrauterine devices, procedures for sterilization, and national family planning methods."[308] These guidelines from his work on family planning programs were made available to public health authorities by WHO. These included studies on the effects of oral contraceptives on malnourished women, the side effects of injectable contraceptives, the effectiveness of natural family planning methods, and the relative advantages of different abortion techniques.[309] The Director-General also announced the continuation of research on synthetic contraceptive chemicals begun in 1976, funded directly by WHO and indirectly by the *US National Institutes of Health*.[310] In 1986,

[304] *Id.* at 7.
[305] *Id.* at 9.
[306] *Id.* at 7 & chart p.8.
[307] A33/9, *supra* note 139, at 22 § 11.
[308] A34/3, *supra* note 250, at 23 § 102.
[309] A33/9, *supra* note 139, at 22 § 8.
[310] A34/3, *supra* note 250, at 24 § 103.

we also learned that large-scale clinical trials had begun on various contraceptives.[311]

In 1994, other technologies had also continued to be developed and evaluated. These included intrauterine devices, emergency contraception (based on mifepristone), and natural family planning methods.[312] In 1993, the Executive Director reported that several guides on family planning had been published during the year. This included a guide to female sterilization[313] and a brochure on natural family planning methods.[314]

In 1998, the program continued to develop, evaluate and disseminate new methods of fertility regulation and family planning. This included the development of a daily anti-progestational pill (mifepristone), a quarterly contraceptive injection (levonorgestrel butanoate), emergency contraception, non-surgical abortion and quarterly injections for men.[315]

Intrauterine devices

Since 1972, the objective of the HRP has been to evaluate the safety and efficacy of the various models of intrauterine devices (IUDs) that exist through clinical trials. As a result, a task force has been researching

---

[311] World Health Organization [WHO], A40/3, *Report of the Director-General on the work of WHO in 1986*, (Feb. 18, 1987), *in* 40th World Health Assembly, Geneva, 4-15 May 1987 - Resolutions and Decisions, Annex 6, at 90, 98 (1987), at §127 https://apps.who.int/iris/bitstream/handle/10665/163285/WHA40_3_eng.pdf?sequence=1&isAllowed=y [hereinafter *A40/3*]

[312] WHO, *Challenges in Reproductive Health Research: Biennial Report: 1992-1993*, at 9-20 (1994), https://apps.who.int/iris/handle/10665/39653 [hereinafter *Challenges, Biennial Report: 1992-1993*].

[313] WHO, *Female Sterilization: a Guide to the Provision of Services*, (Geneva, 1992) https://apps.who.int/iris/handle/10665/40133.

[314] World Health Organization [WHO], WHO/MCH/FPP/92.3, *Natural Family Planning Methods: What Health Workers Need to Know*, § 70 (1993), https://apps.who.int/iris/handle/10665/65252.

[315] World Health Organization [WHO], *Reproductive Health Research, the New Directions, Biennial Report: 1996-1997*, (1998), https://apps.who.int/iris/handle/10665/42105?locale-attribute=pt&. [hereinafter *Biennial Report 1996-1997*]

methods of regulating implantation through the development of medicated intrauterine devices (IUDs) since 1973.[316] Another goal was to prepare evidence-based guidelines on these devices for providers. Between 1972 and 2007, this work resulted in 63 clinical trials and studies that yielded 156 publications, constituting the bulk of the world's scientific evidence on IUDs safety and effectiveness. In particular, the HRP was able to determine the safety and duration of contraceptive effect of copper-bearing IUDs and their mode of action. The 1994 release by the U.S. *Food and Drug Administration* of 10 years of registration data for the TCu380A device[317] was an important milestone in HRP's IUDs activity. According to the HRP, TCu380A acts primarily by preventing fertilization. The research also aimed to develop universally acceptable, evidence-based guidelines for service delivery. This resulted in various publications[318] and eventually the recognition of TCu380A as a highly effective long-term contraceptive method. The evaluation estimates that the HRP was a major contributor to an increase from 70 million to 160 million IUDs users between 1972 and 2007. It also estimates that the expanded use of these IUDs "can have a major impact on global health and economy." [319]

Implantable hormonal devices and injectable contraceptives

In 1973, other *Task forces* were also working on injectable contraceptives with the goal of developing "safe, simple, and effective" methods of

---

[316] *HR/73.5a, supra* note 245, at 12.

[317] In 2001, studies also showed the efficacy and safety of the copper IUD TCu-380A World Health Organization [WHO], *Research on Reproductive Health at WHO, Biennial Report: 2000-2001,* at 14-15 (2002), https://apps.who.int/iris/bitstream/handle/10665/42505/9241562080_eng.pdf?sequence=1&isAllowed=y [hereinafter *Biennial Report 2000-2001*].

[318] *"Medical eligibility criteria for contraceptive use (MEC)* – third edition[;] *Selected practice recommendations for contraceptive use*[;] *Decision-making tool for family planning clients and providers*[;] and *"Family planning: a global handbook for providers."* World Health Organization [WHO], *External Evaluation 2003-2007: Executive Summary,* at 4 (2008), https://apps.who.int/iris/handle/10665/69889.

[319] World Health Organization [WHO], *External Evaluation 2003-2007: Long-term Safety and Effectiveness of Copper-releasing Intrauterine Devices: Case Study,* at 1-2 (2008), https://apps.who.int/iris/handle/10665/69908.

fertility control by injecting compounds at intervals of three months or more.[320] Several years later, in 1990, the CEO announced the successful completion of clinical development of several contraceptives, including the monthly injections *Cyclofem* and *Mesigyna,* and a levonorgestrel-release ring.[321] In 1994, it was also confirmed that, in collaboration with the pharmaceutical industry, the programme had developed two once-a-month injectable combination products (*Cyclofem* and *Mesigyna*) that had a very effective prolonged contraceptive action.[322] The *Concept Foundation,* in collaboration with the *Program for Appropriate Technology in Health* (PATH), had also supported technology transfer for the production of *Cyclofem* in Indonesia, Mexico and Thailand, and distribution agreements had been reached for most Latin American countries.[323] By 1994, WHO-supported trials had been completed in Mexico and were continuing in other countries (Chile, Indonesia, Jamaica, Thailand, and Tunisia) for a once-a-month injectable contraceptive.[324]

In 1998, the programme tested the *Norplant* subcutaneous contraceptive implant with support from *Family Health International* and the *Population Council.*[325] In 2001, the HRP reported that studies of 15,000 women in eight developing countries showed the efficacy and safety of the implantable contraceptive *Norplant* with levonorgestrel.[326] In 2003, the HRP then launched a randomized controlled trial of the implantable contraceptives *Jadelle* and *Implanon.* This trial was conducted in seven countries on 2000 women and the results were expected by the end of 2008.[327] In 2010, the Jadelle and Implanon implantable hormonal contraceptive safety, efficacy, and acceptability trial continued, with

---

[320] *HR/73.5a, supra* note 245, at 20-21.

[321] *Biennial Report 1988-1989, supra* note 185.

[322] *Challenges, Biennial Report: 1992-1993, supra* note 312, at 18.

[323] *Id.* at 22.

[324] WHO A46/3, *Report of the Director-General on the work of WHO,* (Apr. 7, 1993), *in* 46th World Health Assembly, Geneva, 3-14 May 1993, Resolutions and Decisions, annex 13 at 168-69 (1993), https://apps.who.int/iris/handle/10665/176262?locale-attribute=ru&.

[325] *Biennial Report: 1996-1997, supra* note 315, at 50, 59.

[326] *Biennial Report 2000-2001, supra* note 317, at 7.

[327] *Biennial Report 2006-2007, supra* note 10, at 12.

two of the seven centers completing the five-year follow-up.[328] In 2014, a clinical trial of the hormonal contraceptive implants *Jadelle*® (75 mg levonorgestrel) and *Implanon*® (68 mg etonogestrel) had shown their effectiveness and safety.[329]

A 2004 report indicates that the HRP had been conducting basic implantation research for five years in collaboration with the *Rockefeller Foundation*, with the goal of developing an anti-implantation agent that would be less expensive and have fewer side effects. Work on various methods had been conducted at six centers in Australia, China, Germany, India, the United Kingdom and the United States. In May 2003, a meeting was held to present the results of this research. The pharmaceutical industry was invited to discuss potential collaborations.[330]

Sterilization

In 1972, a *Task Force* on methods of regulation of ovum transport was working to develop a variety of agents and methods that interfere with the transport and/or survival of the ovum. Several lines of research were identified for this purpose. These included the development of new chemical of occluding the fallopian tubes by non-surgical means. This was considered to be a promising approach to fertility regulation: "The potential acceptability of a simple, safe, irreversible method of sterilization carried out as a single visit outpatient procedure, among women who have achieved their desired family size is obvious."[331] In 1973, the Task Force on methods of regulation of ovum transport aimed to develop new methods of occluding the oviducts (fallopian tubes) and interfering with ovum survival.[332]

---

[328] WHO, *HRP Highlights of 2010*, at 5 (2011), https://apps.who.int/iris/handle/10665/70726 [hereinafter *HRP Highlights of 2010*].
[329] WHO, *HRP Highlights of 2014*, (2015), https://apps.who.int/iris/handle/10665/153841 [hereinafter *Highlights of 2014*].
[330] *Biennial Report 2002-2003*, *supra* note 9, at 17.
[331] HR/72.5a, *supra* note 134, at 10.
[332] *Id.* at 6.

In 2008, the HRP organized a technical consultation in collaboration with *Family Health International* on the use of quinacrine hydrochloride pellets inserted into the uterus for non-surgical sterilization. This consultation was to evaluate the safety criteria and cancer risks associated with the administration of this molecule. It was decided that until data was available, quinacrine should not be used, including in a clinical or research setting. The WHO expected to give an opinion in 2009 on the safety of quinacrine for non-surgical sterilization of women.[333] There is no further information on this subject since. It should also be noted that quinacrine has a very bad reputation. For example, in 1998, the Indian Supreme Court called the government "to order for having turned a blind eye to tens of thousands of quinacrine sterilizations performed in the country for over a decade."[334]

Contraceptive vaccines

In 1972, a *Task Force* on research into methods of regulating implantation sought to develop methods to prevent or disrupt the implantation of the fertilized egg in the uterus. Two methods were proposed for this purpose. First, the development of medicated intrauterine devices releasing active principles at a constant rate over long periods (which had been the subject of a *Task Force* since the 1970s). Second, the development of immunological methods: "There is evidence from work in animals and humans that the uterus and placenta contain and secrete proteins specific to the reproductive system. If these proteins can be identified, it is possible that their action could be blocked by immunological techniques".[335] Until then, serious reactions caused by the adjuvants used and non-specific antibody reactions against other organs of the body were a problem. But, according to this paper published in 1972: "In recent years, new developments in this field have demonstrated that highly purified

---

333 WHO, *HRP Highlights of 2008*, at 1 (2009), https://apps.who.int/iris/handle/10665/70062.

334 *Stérilisations indiennes* [Indian Sterilizations], LA RECHERCHE, (June 1998) https://www.larecherche.fr/stérilisations-indiennes.

335 HR/72.5a, *supra* note 134, at 12.

human proteins can be chemically altered and made antigenic in humans, thereby avoiding previous obstacles. The *Task Force* is considering a programme of research to isolate specific proteins from the human endometrium, uterine fluid and from early placentae. Specific antibodies against these proteins would then be studied as a means of preventing and disrupting implantation."[336]

Immunological methods that interfere with implantation were thus assigned in 1973 to a new *Task Force* on immunological methods for fertility regulation. The objective of this *Task Force* was to develop immunological methods to prevent or disrupt implantation, to prevent sperm transport and fertilization and to prevent hatching of the blastocyst (5/6-day old embryo) by interference with the zona pellucida (egg shell membrane). The principle behind this work was to isolate specific proteins from the reproductive system to block their action through immunological techniques. The WHO did not expect that all trails of research in this area would be successful and anticipated that it would take eight to fifteen years to bring one of the trails to get to the stage of a marketable vaccine.[337] Nonetheless, research costs were estimated for five vaccines: Human chorionic gonadotropin (HCG) (β-subunit) vaccine (US$99,000 in 1973 - US$210,000 for 1976); Human chorionic sommato-mammotrophin (HCS) vaccine (US$39,800 in 1973 - US$130,000 for 1975); Zona pellucida vaccine (US$34,700 in 1973 - US$250,000 for 1976); Sperm vaccine (US$114,500 in 1973 - US$400,000 for 1976); Trophoblast vaccine (US$460,000 in 1974 - US$400,000 for 1976).[338]

---

[336] *Id.* at 12-13.
[337] *HR/73.5a, supra* note 245, at 17-19.
[338] World Health Organization [WHO], HR/73.5c, *Expanded Programme of Research, Development and Research Training in Human Reproduction: projections 1974-1976, November 1973*, at 8 (1973), https://apps.who.int/iris/handle/10665/361197.

In a report published in 1987,[339] the Director-General reported on research into vaccines for fertility regulation[340]: "The Special Programme has developed and brought into Phase I clinical trials an almost totally synthetic birth control vaccine, after obtaining permission from both the United States *Food and Drug Administration* and the Australian *Drug Regulatory Authority*."[341] Another 1986 report by the Executive Director also confirms that clinical trials had begun on a birth control vaccine developed by the Programme that was undergoing initial clinical trials in Australia.[342] An article from 1986 also refers to these trials,[343]stating that thirty women had volunteered to participate in the human experimentation of a synthetic contraceptive vaccine in the Australian city of Adelaide : "The vaccine was developed by Ohio State University (USA), in collaboration with other academic institutions, the pharmaceutical industry and the WHO." This vaccine worked against a hormone produced shortly after fertilization and thus prevented nesting. It had already been shown to be effective in baboons before this trial was conducted. In June 1989, a symposium was held on the evaluation of the safety and efficacy of vaccines to regulate fertility.[344]

---

[339] EB81/22, *supra* note 176.

[340] *Id.* at 6: "The vaccine consists of a synthetic carboxyterminal 109-145 aminoacid region of the β-subunit of human chorionic gonadotropin, conjugated to diphtheria toxoid as the carrier, administered with muramyl dipeptide adjuvant in a squalene-arlacel vehicle. The development of a second generation vaccine is also in progress."

[341] *Id.* at 5. §6.3. *See also* WHO, *Report: Meeting of the Policy and Coordination Advisory Committee (PCAC), Geneva, 20-22 May 1987*, annex 4 at 33-34 (1987), https://apps.who.int/iris/bitstream/handle/10665/61498/HRP_PCAC%284%29_1987.pdf?sequence=1&isAllowed=y.

[342] A40/3, *supra* note 311, at 90, 98.

[343] Rouzé Michel, *Plus fort que la pilule : le vaccin contraceptif* [*Stronger than the Pill: the contraceptive vaccine*], RAISON PRÉSENTE, at 143 (1986), https://www.persee.fr/doc/raipr_0033-9075_1986_num_79_1_2536_t1_0143_0000_2.

[344] *Biennial Report 1988-1989*, *supra* note 185.

In 1989, the Director-General also reported on the activities of the Expanded Programme on Immunization.[345] He reports that, after receiving grants from the *Rockefeller Foundation*, the UNDP and the Netherlands, this Programme was given the task of complementing the more basic research work carried out in the framework of other WHO programmes, including the Special Programme for Research in Human Reproduction.[346]

According to the HRP biannual report for the years 1992-1993,[347] fertility-regulating vaccines were still being developed for use by women to provide long-term, but not permanent, contraceptive protection while avoiding the menstrual cycle disruption and metabolic side effects associated with hormonal methods.[348] A Phase II clinical trial of the prototype human chorionic gonadotropin (hCG) vaccine developed by the Programme was launched in two centers in Sweden in December 1993. Research also led to progress in developing an optimized version of this type of vaccine that would be less expensive, easier to produce, and potentially more effective than existing formulations. In addition, preliminary studies had been conducted to determine the feasibility of taking such a vaccine orally and to assess its safe reversibility on demand.[349]

The HRP's bi-annual report for the years 1996-1997[350] summarized the developments and status of research on this vaccine since 1973 and its mechanisms of action. This form of contraception sought to block nesting by making the body produce antibodies circulating in the blood that neutralize the action of a hormone, human chorionic gonadotropin (hCG), which is produced from the 7th day after fertilization of the egg.

---

[345] World Health Organization [WHO], A42/10, *Expanded Programme on Immunization, Progress and Evaluation Report*, *in* 42d World Health Assembly, Geneva, 8-13 May 1989, Part I: Resolutions and Decisions, annex 6 at 135 (1989), https://apps.who.int/iris/handle/10665/171211?locale-attribute=fr&.

[346] *Id.* at § 6.18.

[347] *Challenges, Biennial Report: 1992-1993*, *supra* note 312.

[348] *Id.* at 9.

[349] *Id.* at 18.

[350] *Biennial Report: 1996-1997*, *supra* note 315, at 29-30.

The fertilized egg is then expelled. It is a durable method without being permanent (it stops when the level of anti-hCG antibodies in the blood decreases), while avoiding the side effects associated with hormonal methods. Several clinical trials have been conducted to test this vaccine. The first one took place in Australia between 1986 and 1988 on 43 volunteers. Its goal was to evaluate the safety of the vaccine (phase I safety trials). No serious adverse events were reported. Another Phase II efficacy trial was then launched in Sweden in 1993, but it was interrupted due to an adverse event not detected in the Australian trial. Work was then undertaken to change the formulation to avoid this side effect and the trial was scheduled to resume in 1998.[351] The goal was to provide a vaccine with the longest duration of effect (12 months) with the fewest number of injections possible or with oral administration. Studies also aimed to find a way to safely stop and reverse the effect of the vaccine at any time. The report estimated that 5 to 7 years of clinical trials and product improvement were still needed before a first-generation product would be available. Another second-generation synthetic bioengineered product was also in development with a relatively similar estimated time frame for availability (a licensing agreement for the eventual manufacture of this product had been reached between Ohio State University and an industry partner).

According to the HRP report for 2000-2001, the *Population Council* had attempted to develop a vaccine based on the hCG protein, but it had not progressed beyond Phase I. The *National Institute of Immunology* in India had also developed such a vaccine, which reached Phase II. The National Institute of Immunology in India also developed such a vaccine, which reached Phase II. Both attempts were unsuccessful. In contrast, a third vaccine, based on a small fragment of the hCG molecule, was the focus of HRP research in 2001.[352]

---

[351] *See also Id.* at 19-30 (the 1998 report for the years 1996-1997 on contraceptive vaccines).

[352] *Biennial Report 2000-2001, supra* note 317, at 23.

In 2004, the Swedish regulatory authorities approved an application to begin a Phase I trial of a promising molecule, and funding for the trial was secured in late 2005. In 2006, the Programme was still working on an immunocontraceptive for women that could offer about six months of protection after a single injection.[353]

Finally, between 2012-2013, HRP had initiated a phase I trial of immunocontraception with human chorionic gonadotropin (hCG).[354]

It appears that studies on immunocontraception have continued to the present day.[355]

Unsafe abortion and the introduction of medication abortion

In 1972, a Task Force on the use of prostaglandins in fertility regulation aimed to "establish the efficacy, safety and acceptability of prostaglandins and their analogues for the interruption of pregnancy between the first and fifth months, and as methods of contraception,"[356] To this end, one line of research was to conduct clinical trials based on the premise that prostaglandins "offer a potential fertility control of special interest to those countries that have accepted interruption of pregnancy as a method of approach to birth control."[357] The goal was to "develop safe, simple, and effective methods" for second-trimester abortions, abortions between the sixth and twelfth weeks, and to

---

[353] World Health Organization [WHO], *Sexual and Reproductive Health: Laying the Foundation for a more just World through Research and Action, Biennial Report 2004-2005,* at 14 (2006), https://apps.who.int/iris/handle/10665/43497.

[354] World Health Organization [WHO], *WHO Sexual and Reproductive Health Medium-term Strategic Plan for 2010-2015 and Programme Budget for 2012-2013*, at 67 (2011), https://apps.who.int/iris/handle/10665/78068.

[355] *See generally* Kiranjeet Kaur & Vijay Prabha, *Immunocontraceptives: New Approaches to Fertility Control,* 2014 BIOMED RSCH. INT'L (July 10, 2014), https://www.researchgate .net/figure/Immunocontraception-using-an-immune-response-to-zona-pellucida-ZP-The-immune-response_fig2_264676466?fbclid=IwAR1zYkZUY508JQJ6bWchkanL GV0Ai6mcwsJ-NRAr-c1IrYgIQxduxAzYEGM; *and* Search results for "Immunocontraception," PUBMED, https://pubmed.ncbi.nlm.nih.gov/?term= immunocontraception (last visited July 3, 2023).

[356] HR/72.5a, *supra* note 134, at 18.

[357] *Id.*

achieve cervical dilation prior to aspiration. Trials were conducted around the world to determine the ideal dosages for inducing abortion.[358] In 1977, a report also noted that "the value of prostaglandins as a non-surgical and safer method of second-trimester termination of pregnancy has been shown by the Programme, and this research has been essentially completed."[359]

The evaluation of early and late sequelae of abortions was another focus of research. In 1971, it was considered of great importance to conduct an international study on the late sequelae of legal abortions.[360] In 1972, a task force sought to assess the short- and long-term sequelae of induced abortion to "improving the provision of services". The WHO recognized that "very little is known about possible long-term sequelae."[361] The questions of "the health service implications of induced abortion and the psychosocial aspects of pregnancy termination" were also studied.[362] Here, abortion is described "as a fertility regulating method in a number of countries."[363] In June 1972, a meeting was also held to discuss the possible links between the use of hormonal contraceptives and the appearance of chromosomal and anatomical anomalies in what the Director-General calls "the products of subsequent pregnancies."[364]

By 1987, the Special Programme had developed improved abortion techniques for use in the first and second trimesters.[365] That same year, he was also able to determine "which prostaglandin analogue, dose regimen, formulation and route of administration are the most suitable in different clinical situations".[366] In 1990, research had also continued

---

[358] *HR/73.5a, supra* note 245, at 14-16.
[359] EB61/23, *supra* note 247, at 7-15.
[360] HR/71.4 add. 1, *supra* note 145, at 6-7.
[361] HR/72.5a, *supra* note 134, at 22.
[362] *HR/73.5a, supra* note 245, at 22-24.
[363] *HR/71.9 Expanded Programme, supra* note 289.
[364] *Work of WHO 1972, supra* note 242.
[365] EB81/22, *supra* note 176, at 5.
[366] *Id.*

to evaluate the safety and efficacy of the nonsurgical approach to early abortion via administration of an antiprogestin and a prostaglandin.[367]

In 2001, the programme also outlined its work to prevent unsafe abortions. For this purpose, studies were conducted on non-surgical abortion. Eight studies were conducted on more than 6,000 women in 20 countries. They demonstrated the effectiveness of low doses of mifepristone plus a prostaglandin, compared to higher doses.[368] This report also shows that from 2006, a trial was conducted on 3,007 women in 15 centers located in 11 countries, on misoprostol dosages associated with mifepristone to induce abortion up to nine weeks. Results were expected in 2009. Another study conducted in seven countries showed that the use of misoprostol alone was less effective in inducing abortion.[369]

In 2008, a report was published on the impact of the HRP on medical abortion research.[370] The Programme believed that medical abortion was a safe and effective alternative to surgical abortion that could play a role in reducing unsafe abortions. This belief was built on a series of meetings and a review of the published literature on medical abortion. By that year, clinical trials had been conducted, guidelines published, and the use of Medabon® promoted. Between 1999 and 2007, the HRP spent $1.7 million on research on medical abortion (primarily clinical trials). The results were the publication of several studies, the registration of Medabon®, and the addition of mifepristone and misoprostol to the WHO model list of essential medicines. For its trials, HRP collaborated with 15 medical centers and three academic clinical institutions and established a public-private partnership with the *Concept Foundation* and the pharmaceutical company *Sun Pharma* for the

---

367 *Biennial Report 1988-1989, supra* note 185.

368 *Biennial Report 2000-2001, supra* note 317, at 8.

369 World Health Organization [WHO], *HRP Highlights of 2008*, at 3 (2009), https://apps.who.int/iris/handle/10665/70062.

370 World Health Organization [WHO], *External Evaluation 2003-2007: Impact of HRP Research in Medical (Non-surgical) Induced Abortion: a Case Study*, (2008), https://apps.who.int/iris/handle/10665/69907.

registration and production of Medabon®. Medabon®, which combines mifepristone and misoprostol, is less expensive than its two components alone. This low cost led to the expectation that it would be more widely available worldwide, particularly in developing countries, and therefore reduce the number of unsafe abortions, especially surgical ones (the HRP estimated that it could prevent one million unsafe abortions per year and 3,600 maternal deaths per year). The results of the HRP trials were also disseminated to governments to help them develop strategies for introducing medical abortion. In 2008, the Programme also continued to work on the prevention of unsafe abortion, including the development of standards, tools, and guidelines based on available research evidence[371]. The 6th edition of *Unsafe abortion: global and regional estimates of the incidence of unsafe abortion and associated mortality* was published this year[372].This document estimated that 21.6 million unsafe abortions occurred worldwide in 2008 (almost all in developing countries) and that 13% of all maternal deaths were due to unsafe abortions.[373]

In 2008-2009, the HRP also continued its work on the prevention of unsafe abortion by improving the technologies used, working to improve access to abortion in countries, and drafting standards, tools, and guidelines. This work has resulted in several studies, including one that concluded "that the lowest induced abortion rates are associated with high contraceptive prevalence together with liberal abortion laws." A multicenter randomized trial was also conducted on the most effective dosages for the administration of abortive molecules.[374] In 2009, a study was also conducted to map the links between unsafe abortion and maternal mortality for the year 2005. It was determined that unsafe abortion caused 70,500 maternal deaths, all but 60 of which occurred in developed countries. 54% of these deaths occurred in

---

[371] *HRP Highlights of 2010, supra* note 328.
[372] World Health Organization [WHO], *Unsafe Abortion: Global and Regional Estimates of Incidence of Unsafe Abortion and Associated Mortality in 2008*, (6th ed. 2011), https://apps.who.int/iris/handle/10665/44529.
[373] *HRP Highlights of 2010, supra* note 328, at 7.
[374] *HRP 2008-2009, supra* note 186, at 13.

Africa. The Program developed a four-year programme: "Research and action to prevent unsafe abortion." This project aimed to improve abortion technologies, generate data, and support the establishment of safe abortion services. Its results were considered very positive and led to numerous publications.[375] The HRP also worked to help countries improve access to safe abortion and quality post-abortion care. A trial in Nepal had shown that trained nurses and auxiliary midwives could perform first-trimester medical abortion as safely as doctors. A clinical practice guideline for safe abortion care was field tested in Ethiopia and Nepal and published in 2014.[376] Technical support was also provided to Guinea, Malawi, Russia, and Senegal, including improving access to comprehensive abortion care.[377] As of 2011, twenty-five research projects (clinical and operational) either had been completed or were underway in this area. A statistical paper on abortion had also been published in The Lancet: "*Induced abortion: incidence and trends worldwide from 1995 to 2008.*"[378]

In 2012, the HRP stated that to prevent unsafe abortion, WHO wanted to emphasize better access to and use of contraception; sex education and management of complications; and access to safe and legal abortions. To work in this area, the department thus published in June 2012 the second edition of *Safe abortion technical and policy guidance for health systems*[379] that "presents new evidence-based recommendations on clinical care, service- delivery strengthening, and human rights and legal considerations." Three workshops were held in the African, Southeast Asian, and European regions to disseminate the guidelines, and a subregional workshop involving 10 African countries was held in Kenya to develop detailed country implementation strategies. The

---

[375] World Health Organization [WHO], *HRP Highlights 2009,* at 3 (2010), https://apps.who.int/iris/handle/10665/70347.

[376] World Health Organization [WHO], *Clinical Practice Guideline for Safe Abortion Care,* (2014), https://apps.who.int/iris/handle/10665/97415.

[377] *HRP Highlights of 2010, supra* note 328, at.9.

[378] *Id.* at 12.

[379] World Health Organization [WHO], *Safe Abortion: Technical and Policy Guidance for Health Systems,* (2d ed., 2012), https://apps.who.int/iris/handle/10665/70914.

results of two clinical trials were also published. The first showed that cervical preparation with misoprostol reduced the incidence of complications for vacuum aspiration abortion in the first trimester (published in *The Lancet*). The second study examined the acceptability of medical abortion with misoprostol alone. It showed that in comparison to surgical abortion, "the women who chose misoprostol-only medical abortion were more likely to be 'satisfied' or 'highly satisfied' with the procedure (published in the *British Journal of Obstetrics and Gynaecology*)".[380]

In 2012, two HRP-led clinical trials published in *The Lancet* demonstrated that trained nurses and midwives can perform surgical and nonsurgical abortions as safely as physicians. The Programme also "played a catalytic role in the development of medical abortion." This is particularly the case "in developing a low-cost formulation of safe and effective medical abortion regimen for the first-trimester (comprising mifepristone and misoprostol)." Technical and policy guidelines were also published as a reference document for UN organizations, NGOs, professional associations, programme managers, and health care providers.[381]

In 2013, the HRP believed that barriers to safe abortion care included a lack of standards and guidelines and inadequate training for abortion providers. Other situations also seen as a barrier to prevention included limited access to contraception, gender inequality, and limited access to sex education.[382] In 2015, a guideline on *Health worker roles in providing safe abortion care and post-abortion contraception* was published[383] with an interactive website to facilitate access to these recommendations[384]. A study also found that the provision of medical abortions by midwives

---

[380] World Health Organization [WHO], *HRP Highlights of 2012*, at 13-14 (2013), https://apps.who.int/iris/handle/10665/85154.
[381] *HRP at 40, supra* note 218, at 13-14.
[382] *External Evaluation 2008-2012, supra* note 1, at 26-27.
[383] WHO, *Health Worker Roles in Providing Safe Abortion Care and Post-Abortion Contraception*, (2015) https://apps.who.int/iris/handle/10665/181041.
[384] This website can be found at http://srhr.org/safeabortion/.

in rural areas of Kyrgyzstan was "safe, effective and feasible." Preliminary data collection on abortion laws and policies had also been completed in 190 countries.[385]

In 2016, HRP defined unsafe abortion as the situation where "a pregnancy is terminated either by persons lacking the necessary skills or in an environment that does not conform to minimal medical standards, or both." He went on to explain that the rate of unsafe abortions is higher when there is limited or no access to effective contraception and safe abortion care. This is estimated to account for 22 million abortions per year worldwide, causing nearly 22,000 deaths. The HRP estimated that in addition to these deaths and disabilities, unsafe abortions have a significant social and financial cost to women, families, communities, and health systems. In July 2016, HRP and researchers from the *Guttmacher Institute* published a statistical study in *The Lancet* on the incidence of abortion between 1990 and 2014. This study showed a 41% decline in the incidence of abortion in developed regions. It also showed that this decline did not occur in developing countries where 88% of abortions performed worldwide took place.[386]

In 2018, HRP oversaw a six-country study (Colombia, Ethiopia, Ghana, Portugal, South Africa, and Uruguay) on the impact of legal reform on the prevention of unsafe abortion (published in the *International Journal of Gynecology & Obstetrics*). The HRP staff also published a systematic review "on the magnitude and severity of abortion-related morbidity in settings with limited access to abortion services."[387] The HRP director explained that medical abortion "plays an important role in helping to ensure safe, effective, and acceptable abortion care, when given or supported by a trained provider." In an effort to improve access, in 2018, the HRP launched the "combi-pack" which aimed to foster

---

[385] World Health Organization [WHO], *HRP Highlights of 2015*, at 8 (2016), https://apps.who.int/iris/handle/10665/206544 [hereinafter *HRP Highlights of 2015*].
[386] *Annual Report 2016*, *supra* note 7, at 12-13 https://apps.who.int/iris/handle/10665/255768
[387] World Health Organization [WHO], *HRP Annual Report 2018*, at 16 (2019), https://apps.who.int/iris/handle/10665/310956.

collaboration between governments, donors, UN agencies, NGOs, social marketing organizations, and manufacturers of medical abortion products with the goal of disseminating combined mifepristone and misoprostol kits. The HRP collaborated in particular with the *Concept Foundation* for this purpose. A new guideline "to help health-care workers ensure access to safe medical abortion care, Medical management of abortion"[388] was also published.[389] In 2019, in an effort to combat unsafe abortion, the HRP had mifepristone and misoprostol added to the *WHO Model List of Essential Medicines.*[390]

Finally, in 2020, a study[391] published in *The Lancet Global Health* by the *Guttmacher Institute* and HRP showed a global decline in unintended pregnancies since 1990-1994 and an increase in the proportion of unintended pregnancies ending in abortion. This is viewed positively as a demonstration of improved access to family planning and contraceptive services. However, the study found that between 2015 and 2019, nearly half of all pregnancies were unplanned, three times more in the poorest regions than in the richest regions.[392]

Emergency contraception

In 1972, one line of research was the development of a pill that could be taken after sexual intercourse, particularly in the case of "emergency use." In concrete terms, this was the development of the "morning-after pill." The objective at the time was to find a method that was better tolerated and had fewer side effects than the high-dose estrogen method that had been used until then.[393] A 1994 report shows that

---

[388] *Id.*

[389] World Health Organization [WHO], *Medical Management of Abortion,* (2018) https://apps.who.int/iris/bitstream/handle/10665/278968/9789241550406-eng.pdf.

[390] World Health Organization [WHO], *HRP Annual Report 2019,* at 12-13 (2020), https://apps.who.int/iris/handle/10665/331637.

[391] WHO, *New estimates show worldwide fall in unintended pregnancies since 1990-1994,* WHO NEWS (July 23, 2020), https://www.who.int/news/item/23-07-2020-new-estimates-show-worldwide-fall-in-unintended-pregnancies-since-1990-1994.

[392] *HRP Annual Report 2020, supra* note 8, at 19.

[393] HR/72.5a, *supra* note 134, at 10.

emergency contraception (based on mifepristone) had continued to be developed and evaluated over the following years.[394]

In 2008, the HRP funded 24 studies on quality of care in sexual and reproductive health services. A trial in Nigeria compared the efficacy and side effects of levonorgestrel as an emergency contraceptive with the doses administered. A similar study was conducted in China with the TCu380A IUD.[395] It was concluded in 2010 that this intrauterine device was safe and effective for emergency contraception.[396] In 2010, a study conducted at a family planning center in Chile also showed that levonorgestrel emergency contraception only prevents pregnancy when taken before fertilization.[397] In 2012, the HRP believed it had played a "pioneering role" in the development of emergency contraception leading to its use in 140 countries. In particular, the Programme had conducted a large trial demonstrating the safety and effectiveness of levonorgestrel for this purpose. Noting that one of the obstacles to its use was the fear of its abortifacient effect, the HRP also conducted a review of the scientific literature that showed that levonorgestrel disrupts ovulation and prevents fertilization. This review therefore stated that "Levonorgestrel emergency contraceptives do not interrupt an established pregnancy or harm a developing embryo."[398] In 2013, a report also stated that levonorgestrel can prevent pregnancy if taken within 120 hours of intercourse. It again stated that the molecule was not abortifacient and claimed that it was safe for over-the-counter use. The HRP thus encouraged its distribution through "social marketing."[399]

---

394 *Challenges, Biennial Report: 1992-1993*, *supra* note 312, at 20.

395 World Health Organization [WHO], *HRP Highlights of 2008*, at 3 (2009), https://apps.who.int/iris/handle/10665/70062.

396 *HRP 2008-2009*, *supra* note 186, at 6.

397 *HRP Highlights of 2010*, *supra* note 328, at 5.

398 *HRP at 40*, *supra* note 218, at 11.

399 *External Evaluation 2008-2012*, *supra* note 1, at 29.

The development of male contraceptives

In 1971, the Director-General discussed the progress and growth of vasectomy but, noting the lack of knowledge about basic male reproductive processes, stressed that no viable modern solution had been found for male contraception.[400] In 1972, *Task Forces* wanted to develop methods to regulate the fertilizing power of spermatozoa[401] as well as the migration and survival of spermatozoa.[402]

In 1986, the WHO had "produced technical guidelines on the role in family planning care of barrier methods and spermicides, and on technical and managerial aspects of vasectomy services."[403] Four years later, in 1990, it was announced that research had progressed on the development of a hormonal contraceptive for men.[404] In 1994, the HRP reported on the positive development of hormonal methods for male contraception and the release of a video funded in 1993 by the *Association for Voluntary Surgical Contraception* and the *Program for Appropriate Technology in Health* (PATH) to teach health professionals about non-scalpel vasectomy.[405]

In 2006, research continued on a hormonal contraceptive for men. The HRP oversaw clinical trials in the field and studies on the acceptability of the method. For example, 1,045 men were enrolled in a four-year Phase III study in China to evaluate the effects of a monthly injection of 500 mg of testosterone undecanoate (TU). Nearly a third of these people withdrew from the study because of various side effects.[406] Nevertheless, in 2009, the HRP announced that the phase III trial had

---

[400] *Work of WHO 1971, supra* note 123, at 132-36 § 8.29.
[401] HR/72.5a, *supra* note 134, at 14.
[402] *Id.* at 16.
[403] A40/3, *supra* note 311, at 90, 98.
[404] *Biennial Report 1988-1989, supra* note 185, at 4.
[405] *Challenges, Biennial Report: 1992-1993, supra* note 312, at 19.
[406] World Health Organization [WHO], *Sexual and Reproductive Health: Laying the Foundation for a more just World through Research and Action, Biennial Report 2004-2005,* at 14 (2006), https://apps.who.int/iris/handle/10665/43497.

concluded that this molecule was safe, effective and acceptable.[407] In 2010, a report gave the same conclusion on this contraceptive for a population of Chinese couples.[408] That same year, another study demonstrated the contraceptive efficacy and safety of norethisterone enanthate plus testosterone undeconoate (TU) as an injectable male contraceptive.[409]

According to the evaluation report on HRP activities between 2008 and 2012,[410] a phase II trial was conducted in eight countries on two long-acting injectable hormones for male contraception. However, it had been stopped in April 2012 due to adverse side effects. In 2014, a trial showed the efficacy of norethisterone enanthate and testosterone undecanoate for male contraception, but the high frequency of serious adverse effects needed to be reviewed before further research could be conducted.[411]

Behavioral studies to make contraception acceptable

As early as 1971, with reference to resolution WHA21.43 of 1968, work was proposed on psychological factors related to the health aspects of human reproduction.[412] This was included in the research priorities set by WHO that year. The Programme was to determine the acceptability of various approaches to fertility regulation under different cultural and socioeconomic conditions. The main objective was to identify the conditions under which contraception versus abortion are accepted.[413] A *Task force* was devoted to studying the acceptability of fertility regulation methods in various socio-cultural contexts.[414] Its objective was to advance the practice of family planning by making available new

---

[407] World Health Organization [WHO], *HRP Highlights 2009*, at 1 (2010), https://apps.who.int/iris/handle/10665/70347.
[408] *HRP 2008-2009, supra* note 186.
[409] *HRP Highlights of 2010, supra* note 328, at 5.
[410] *External Evaluation 2008-2012, supra* note 1.
[411] *Highlights of 2014, supra* note 329.
[412] *Work of WHO 1971, supra* note 123.
[413] HR/71.4 add. 1, *supra* note 145, at 4.
[414] HR/72.5a, *supra* note 134, at 12.

methods of fertility regulation adapted to different contexts and cultures.[415] Acceptability was thus seen as a critical element in the success of family planning programmes that require "continuous coverage of a substantial part of the population."[416]

On this question of acceptability, a 1977 report states that "more innovative studies are being conducted, at the specific request of governments, on performance of female sterilization by theatre nurses and vasectomy by medical students."[417] A 1977 document also raised the issue of the acceptability of male and female sterilization by non-physician personnel.[418] WHO also sought the best methods to make various family planning services in developing countries "safer, more effective, simpler and more acceptable". These techniques ranged from oral contraceptives and periodic abstinence methods to sterilization and abortion techniques. The Organization sought to make available to family planning programs new methods that it imagined would be more widely accepted, such as abortifacient drugs, male medicated contraceptives, and vaccines.[419]

In 1986, the programme also continued its research on family planning and the social and behavioural aspects of fertility regulation practices.[420] In 1988, the programme organized an international conference entitled: "Ethics and human values in family planning: an inter-cultural (international) dialogue on rights and responsibilities of individuals and societies regarding reproductive decisions."[421]

In 1994, an HRP report noted that the issue of social attitudes toward contraceptive use had been the subject of social science research. It was found that women who said they did not want more children did not

---

[415] *HR/73.5a, supra* note 245, at 23.
[416] EB61/23, *supra* note 247, at 11.
[417] A30/9, *supra* note 157, annex 3 at 3.
[418] EB61/23, *supra* note 247, at 15.
[419] A30/9, *supra* note 157, annex 3 at 4.
[420] A40/3, *supra* note 311, at 90, 98.
[421] EB81/22, *supra* note 176, at 9.

use contraception even though they were aware of its existence. According to these studies, this choice is influenced by various factors such as women's education, access to services and information, and residence in an urban area. However, given the difficulty of generalizing these results, it was considered important to discover which factors were more important than others in different societies and to translate these findings into policy action.[422]

In 2001, a report stressed the importance of social science research to analyze "behavioural and social underpinnings of sexual and reproductive behaviour and reproductive ill-health." The Programme thus invests "heavily in a large number of social science studies probing the "mysteries" of adolescent sexual and reproductive behaviour in a wide variety of cultural contexts." [423]

The Chinese example

The Programme has worked with China since 1979 to strengthen reproductive health research and is highly respected there. The HRP has played a particularly important role in improving the safety and effectiveness of locally produced contraceptives in China. In China, the stainless-steel ring was the IUD used by about 110 million women, constituting about 50% of contraceptive methods. The HRP was involved in the removal of the IUD and some of the monthly oral contraceptives because it was considered less effective and dangerous. A study was conducted to this end in 1991-1992; it outlined the benefits and health cost savings of switching to copper-T IUDs (TCu 220C and TCu 380A) and subsequently recommended the change.[424]

---

422 *Challenges, Biennial Report: 1992-1993, supra* note 312, at 10.
423 *Biennial Report 2000-2001, supra* note 317, at 6-7.
424 World Health Organization [WHO], *External Evaluation 2003-2007: Improving the Safety and Effectiveness of Contraception in China: a Case-study in Promotion and Improvement of Family Planning*, at 1 (2008), https://apps.who.int/iris/handle/10665/69909.

One report[425] explains that China saw itself as playing an important role for the world through its birth control program, which contributed greatly to the control of world population growth. This view had not always existed. Since 1949 many members of Mao Zedong's government argued that a large population was a good thing and were therefore opposed to contraception. This pro-natalist policy was abandoned in the mid-1950s with the approval and subsequent advocacy of birth control to lift China's large population out of poverty through the provision of low-cost contraceptives and the easing of restrictions against abortion and sterilization. WHO was the first UN agency to establish an office in China in 1979. The HRP was also the first WHO program to send a mission there to address the country's family planning needs. The emphasis was on supporting clinical, biomedical, and social science research in accordance with the highest possible scientific and ethical standards. UNFPA also had an early presence in China, beginning in 1980.[426]

The main partners of the HRP in the country were the National Population and Family Planning Commission and, in terms of research, Shanghai Institute of Planned Parenthood Research (since 1979). This collaboration resulted in a decision in 2004 to withdraw four contraceptives that were problematic in terms of efficacy and safety (the steel and copper rings, the monthly pill, a morning-after pill, and a daily pill). These decisions have also had an impact in India. The HRP estimates that the removal of the steel and copper rings and their replacement with more effective copper IUDs prevented an estimated 1.4 million abortions in 2007.[427]

---

[425] *Id.*

[426] *Id.* at 4.

[427] World Health Organization [WHO], *External Evaluation 2003-2007: Executive Summary*, at 14-16 (2008), https://apps.who.int/iris/handle/10665/69889.

The work of the *Clinical Research Centres*

In 1971, the Expanded Programme provided a document for the evaluation of *Clinical Research Centers* that could collaborate on studies of fertility regulating agents.[428] In 1972, the Regional Director for the WHO Western Pacific Regional Committee explained that, as part of the new WHO Expanded Programme, a worldwide network of research centers being established for collaborative studies evaluating new fertility regulating agents and carrying out comparative trials of existing agents. To this end, WHO human reproduction consultants visited a number of centers in the region.[429]

It was planned in 1973 to increase the number of these *Clinical Research Centres* by two per year until 1976.[430] In that year, this represented 17 institutions in 16 countries, which were created to test new methods developed by the *Task Forces*, independent scientists, or the pharmaceutical industry. A table shows the number of patients recruited for clinical trials in each of the WHO *Clinical Research Centres* in the world. These trials include, for example, the following: Tubal occlusion (Bangkok 30, Chandigarh 30, Singapore 30), Prostaglandins - second trimester abortion (Szeged 100, Los Angeles 500, Chandigarh 350, Mumbai 300, Sydney 50, Stockholm 200), and Prostaglandins - first trimester abortion (Chandigarh 50, Ljubljana 100, Stockholm 100).[431]

---

[428] HR/71.4 add. 1, *supra* note 145, at 145-53.
[429] WHO & Reg'l Comm. W. Pac., WPR/RC23/3,*Twenty-second annual report of the regional director to the regional committee for the western pacific covering the period, 1 July 1971 - 30 June* 1972, at 45-46 (1972), https://apps.who.int/iris/handle/10665/355243?search-result=true&query=WPR%2FRC23%2F3&scope=&rpp=10&sort_by=score&order=desc.
[430]World Health Organization [WHO], HR/73.5c, *Expanded Programme of Research, Development and Research Training in Human Reproduction: projections 1974-1976, November 1973,* (1973), https://apps.who.int/iris/handle/10665/361197?search-result=true&query=%28dc.title%3A%22Expanded+Programme+of+Research%2C+Development+and+Research+Training+in+Human+Reproduction%22%29&scope=%2F&rpp=10&sort_by=score&order=desc.
[431] *HR/73.5a, supra* note 245, at 30.

The work of the four *Research and Training Centres* on human reproduction

In 1972, the WHO *Research and Training Centres* worked on the development of research on fertility regulation. As an example, the Center established at the *Karolinska Institute and Hospital* studied the effects on the human endometrium of different devices, especially copper. It also studied the mechanism of action of chemical agents used to produce tubal occlusion (chemical sterilization). Similarly, the *All Union Scientific Institute of Obstetrics and Gynaecology* in Moscow studied the use of prostaglandins and their analogues in the induction of abortion and labor.[432] In 1973, WHO wanted to promote the multidisciplinary aspect of their work on fertility control and expand their research and training activities in this area. WHO's support for these Centers promoted research on fertility control by involving them in *Task Force* research and by having them collaborate with the *Clinical Research Centers*. To give two examples: the *All-Union Scientific Research Institute of Obstetrics and Gynaecology* in Moscow studied, among other things, the effects of prostaglandins and estrogens on early embryogenesis, while the *Karolinska Institute and Hospital* in Stockholm conducted studies on chemical sterilization methods by tubal occlusion and the effects of copper, gestagens and other substances released into the endometrium by medicated IUDs.[433]

The reasons for and the results of biomedical research

In 1965, World Health Assembly resolution WHA18.49 requested the Director-General to pursue the implementation of a programme that included studies on the medical aspects of infertility and methods of fertility regulation. In 1970, the first meeting of organizations interested in this subject was held, and in 1971, a feasibility report was presented to them. It was validated and funding from several Northern European states and the *Ford Foundation* allowed the implementation of this new

---

[432] HR/72.5a, *supra* note 134, at 29.
[433] *HR/73.5a, supra* note 245, at 32-33.

program. "Hence the idea of a truly neutral, intergovernmental approach towards research, development and research training in human reproduction, with special emphasis on the needs of developing countries, became a reality in 1972".[434] In 1978, the World Health Assembly Resolution WHA31.37 approved the Programme's activities. According to the Director-General, "Although initially it was concern[ed] about demographic development that stimulated interest in family planning, it was rapidly realized that the health aspects of family planning were as important, if not more so. Indeed, WHO does not have a population policy; it is up to Member States to formulate their own policy if they so wish".[435] However, WHO has always had a broad health policy. From its inception, the Special Program recognized that the impact of family planning and fertility regulation went far beyond issues of population growth and expansion. In general, the Executive Director wanted to show that the goal of fertility regulation was to increase the overall health of the population. He also noted that the majority of populations, particularly in developing countries, do not use contraception. According to him, it is because these methods did not always meet their need for "a wide variety of safe and effective methods that will suit the individual situation, the socioeconomic condition, and the cultural and religious values of different couples."[436] He therefore called for an increase "in social, behavioural, and service research to better understand the factors influencing the choice of various methods and their continuation rates."[437]

In 1972, the goal was the development of safe, acceptable, and effective contraceptive technologies while ensuring the long-term safety of existing methods and with the additional goal to "provide support to institutions in developing countries so that they could conduct research relevant to their own needs."[438] In 1979, the Programme had expanded

---

[434] EB81/22, *supra* note 176, at 2.
[435] *Id.* at 2-3.
[436] *Id.* at 3.
[437] *Id.*
[438] *Challenges, Biennial Report: 1992-1993, supra* note 312, at 5.

to include research on the acceptability of various contraceptive methods and on infertility. Finally, in 1988, "reproductive health" became a more general concern with Health Assembly resolution WHA41.9,[439] which approved the mandate of the Special Programme for the Coordination of Global Research in Reproductive Health.[440]

Biomedical research as a tool for population control

In one of his 1989 reports to the World Health Assembly, the Director-General[441] stated that "while WHO does not have an explicit population control policy, the relationship between a balanced population, sufficient food, resources and health is clearly reflected in its programmes. A balanced population and its general state of health are closely interlinked".[442] The Special Programme for Research in Human Reproduction thus aimed at this population balance for economic and general health purposes. In 1972, the Regional Director for the WHO Western Pacific Regional Committee expressed the same idea. Indeed, he reported how the World Bank was interested in financing family planning programs as part of the overall economic development of countries. Multidisciplinary World Bank missions, assisted by WHO staff, visited Malaysia and the Philippines to do just that.[443]

---

[439] World Health Organization [WHO], Res. WHA41.9, *On Special Programme of Research, Development and Research Training in Human Reproduction*, (May 11, 1988), *in* 41st World Health Assembly, Geneva, 2-13 May 1988, Resolutions and Decisions, at 6-7 (1988), https://apps.who.int/iris/handle/10665/164346?search-result=true&query=WHA41.9&scope=&rpp=10&sort_by=score&order=desc.

[440] *Challenges, Biennial Report: 1992-1993*, *supra* note 312, at 5.

[441] World Health Organization [WHO], A/42/9, *WHO's Contribution to the International Efforts towards Sustainable Development, Report of the Director-General*, *in* 42d World Health Assembly, Geneva, 8-13 May 1989, Part I: Resolutions and Decisions, annex 4 at 89, 93 (1989), https://apps.who.int/iris/handle/10665/171211?locale-attribute=fr&.

[442] *Id.* at 89, §13.

[443] WHO & Reg'l Comm. W. Pac., WPR/RC23/3, *Twenty-second Annual Report of the Regional Director to the Regional Committee for the Western Pacific Covering the Period, 1 July 1971 - 30 June 1972*, at 45-46 (1972), https://apps.who.int/iris/handle/10665/355243?search-result=true&query=WPR%2FRC23%2F3&scope=&rpp=10&sort_by=score&order=desc.

In 1995, G. Benagiano and E. Diczfalusy, two former HRP officials, published an article in the *South African Medical Journal* on *Research on Human Reproduction and the United Nations.*[444] The subtitle, *'The French Connection' of Thomas Robert Malthus,* was introduced by a quote from Jean Monnet: "When an idea corresponds to the needs of its time, it ceases to belong to those who invented it and becomes stronger than those who manage it" (Mémoires (1978). In this article, they placed the HRP in a lineage starting with Condorcet, then Malthus and ending with Margaret Sanger:

> It is therefore increasingly being realised today that the global ecosystem imposes limits on the number of people the world can sustain. A Chinese proverb says: "Do not think that you are on the wrong path, simply because you have not gone far enough". Malthus was not wrong… In retrospect, it is clear that Malthus was a brilliant thinker and philosopher. However, he is not the "father" of family planning; the idea of fertility regulation was simply unacceptable to his conventional Christian philosophy. The intellectual father of family planning was the Marquis de Condorcet. Bertrand Russell points out that Condorcet originated Malthus's theory of population, which, however, did not have for him the gloomy consequences that it had for Malthus, because he coupled it with the necessity of active birth control. Malthus's father was a disciple of Condorcet, and it was in this way that Malthus came to know the theory. Interestingly, Condorcet, like the somewhat later Charles Fourier, was also a pioneer in advocating equality for women. William Faulkner says that "the past is never dead; it is not even past…". If Condorcet is the "father" of family planning with its demographic rationale, the "mother" must be Margaret Sanger. She opened her family planning clinic in Brooklyn, New York, on October 16, 1916. It instantly became very popular until, after 11 days, the police department closed it down and Mrs Sanger was sentenced by a

[444] Benagiano & Diczfalusy, *supra* note 6, at 370-73.

> New York court and imprisoned for "obscenity." Mrs Sanger can therefore be considered the "mother" of practical family planning with its human rights and reproductive health rationale.

Reducing fertility in developing countries

In 1971, the Director-General claimed that the African socio-cultural situation prevented the development of an ideal method of fertility regulation.[445] Six years later, while considering the obstacles encountered in the implementation of family planning programmes, particularly in developing countries, he recalled that "the need for research on human reproduction has been stressed in several World Health Assembly resolutions." It was therefore decided to develop a research strategy focused on techniques considered more appropriate to the specific characteristics of these countries.[446] From 1977 onwards, family planning was justified from a health point of view by explaining that it is women and families with the most children who run the greatest health risks, especially in the unfavourable environment of developing countries.[447] However, one report noted that only Western women had been carefully studied for the safety of fertility regulation methods such as the "pill" or "surgical methods of sterilization and abortion techniques." This work has not been done on women in developing countries, taking into account their different lifestyles and environments.[448] Nevertheless, the Director-General noted in 1979, in a way that seems contradictory, that "practically all the research on current methods of fertility regulation, psychosocial and service aspects of family planning, and infertility has been carried out in developing countries".[449] However, this research in developing countries was different from that conducted in developed countries.

---

[445] *Work of WHO 1971, supra* note 123, at 132-36 § 8.29.

[446] A30/9, *supra* note 157.

[447] EB61/23, *supra* note 247, at 11.

[448] A30/9, *supra* note 157, annex 3 at 2.

[449] World Health Organization [WHO], EB65/20, *Development and Coordination of Biomedical and Health Services Research: Report by the Director-General*, § 30 (1979),

In 1980, the Director-General also confirmed the Special Programme's focus on developing countries. Of the 70 countries from which the researchers and research administrators participating in the programme's activities come, 45 were developing countries. The most active collaborating centers for the program were in Argentina, Brazil, Chile, China, Cuba, Egypt, Hong Kong, India, Kenya, Mexico, Nigeria, Pakistan, Philippines, Republic of Korea, Singapore, Sri Lanka, Thailand, Tunisia, Turkey, Viet Nam and Zambia. These researchers had two main objectives. First, building national capacity in human reproductive research in order to strengthen the personnel and research capacity in these countries. Second, promoting research on fertility regulation methods by also studying related aspects (psycho-social aspect, "services" aspect of family planning...).[450] Resolution WHA33.25 of 1980[451] took this report into account, emphasizing in particular the importance of strengthening research in developing countries.

In 1994, the HRP considered that in the context of "a shift in the traditional values associated with sexuality," the provision of information and methods of fertility regulation to adolescents was seen as an important issue, particularly in the face of barriers in societies with "strict traditional customs."[452] That year, for example, the HRP announced that the Programme's goal was to reduce fertility in developing countries to 3.3 births per woman (down from 3.9 in 1985-1990) and to increase contraceptive prevalence to 59%, up from 53% in 1990, in order to reach the UN's average population projection of 6.2 billion by 2000. To achieve this, it was hoped that the number of contraceptive users in developing countries would increase by 186 million by 2000, from 381 million in 1990 to 567 million in 2000.

---

https://apps.who.int/iris/handle/10665/154398?search-result=true&query=EB65%2F20&scope=&rpp=10&sort_by=score&order=desc.

[450] A33/9, *supra* note 139, at 20.

[451] World Health Organization [WHO], Res. WHA33.25, *On Development and Coordination of Biomedical and Health Services Research*, (May 23, 1980), *in* 33d World Health Assembly, Geneva, 5-23 May 1980, resolutions and decisions, at 25-26 (1980), https://apps.who.int/iris/handle/10665/155550?search-result=true&query=WHA33.25&scope=&rpp=10&sort_by=score&order=desc.

[452] *Challenges, Biennial Report: 1992-1993*, *supra* note 312, at 11.

Biomedical research was thus directed toward the goal of expanding contraceptive choice through the development of new methods. These include, for example, male methods and fertility regulating vaccines.[453]

WHO's assessment of the first years of operation of the HRP

In 1971, the Human Reproduction Programme was the largest research programme undertaken by WHO, financially, between basic research, clinical trials of contraceptives, and research training. The Director-General reported to Member States on the results of the programme and on the assistance provided by the programme to governments. For example, in Asia, family planning, which was initially intended to influence population growth, had been transformed into a long-term process integrated with general health services.[454] In response to this presentation, delegates from different countries spoke. For the delegate from the United States, the issue of human reproduction and population dynamics was closely linked to the environmental problem.[455] The delegate from Malawi, while praising the research work to regulate fertility, called for "the attention of the Director-General to the fact that there is still confusion in certain quarters of the world on the difference between family planning for health and population control". Indeed, he felt that "from the literature produced that family planning for health and population control are merely two sides of the same coin". His delegation invited the *Human Reproduction Unit* to clarify the objectives of the programme.[456] Finally, the delegate of the Union of Soviet Socialist Republics rejected the possibility "that

---

[453] *Id.* at 7-9.

[454] World Health Organization [WHO], *Report of the Director-General on the work of WHO in 1971*, 25th World Health Assembly Geneva, 9-26 May 1972, Part II: Plenary Meeting, Verbatim Records at 50-52 (1972), https://apps.who.int/iris/handle/10665/85851?search-result=true&query=Twenty-fifth+World+Health+Assembly%2C+Geneva%2C+9-26+may+1972&scope=&rpp=10&sort_by=score&order=desc

[455] *Id.* at 68.

[456] *Id.* at 82.

study of human reproduction and of methods of reducing the birth rate should become our Organization's largest research programme."[457]

It is also interesting to note a point in Sir George Godber's speech when he was presented with the Leon Bernard Foundation Medal and Prize by the President of WHO at the third session of the World Health Assembly in 1972. For him, the most significant achievement of his twelve years at WHO was "the progressive move into the field of family planning. From being a subject of extreme controversy as lately as 1961 in the Assembly in New Delhi, it has become one of the major fields of activity, especially in research and training; and with the consent of all." He saw in it the "striking example of the capacity of nations to accept change in the manifest interest of world health, even when it threatens to invade subjects once too difficult even for discussion."[458]

In its resolution WHA31.37 of May 1978,[459] the World Health Assembly reaffirmed its commitment to research in human reproduction and approved the objectives of the Special Programme for collaboration with Member States, particularly in the development and application of fertility control techniques. It was also satisfied with the multidisciplinary action groups and the balance between clinical, epidemiological, psycho-social, operational, and laboratory research. It then congratulated "participating Member States and institutions, as well as the Director-General, on the achievements to date of the Special Programme in generating knowledge and technology of immediate social relevance and in promoting self-reliance for research in developing countries". It also invited Member States to support the programme financially and by involving their researchers in it. Finally, the Health Assembly requested the Director-General to intensify the research work of the Special Programme on "health service research in

---

[457] *Id.*at 133.
[458] *Id.* at 256.
[459] WHO Res. WHA31.37, *On Special Programme of Research, Development and Research Training in Human Reproduction*, (May 23, 1978), *in* 31st World Health Assembly Geneva, 8-24 May 1978, Part I Resolutions and Decisions, at 24-25 (1978), https://apps.who.int/iris/handle/10665/93435.

human reproduction [...] as to facilitate the complete integration of services for fertility regulation into the primary health care systems of the countries concerned." It also asked him to continue working on cooperation between the pharmaceutical industry and the WHO.

In 1980, the Director-General recalled the four main objectives of the Special Programme: "strengthening of research capabilities in developing countries; research on the safety of current methods of fertility regulation and development of new methods, on service and psychosocial aspects of family planning care, and on infertility; coordination of world efforts in this field; and dissemination of information to policy makers, service providers, scientists, and the public."[460] This year, various fertility regulation methods were already in advanced stages of development. However, other methods such as long-acting implants and injectables, vaccines, and male fertility regulation methods were not yet developed.[461] In 1986, a study was completed in several countries on the treatment of infertility,[462] and the programme also proposed means of diagnosis and treatment.[463]

In 1987, the Director-General explained that "to fulfil its role, the Special Programme has a broad mandate to carry out research and development, to expand and improve resources for research, to initiate, facilitate, evaluate and coordinate research, and to undertake a number of special responsibilities."[464] These research activities focused on three axes through *Task Forces* that worked under the umbrella of the Special Programme and their own *Steering Committees.*

The first axis was devoted to existing methods. Its first aim was to ensure the safety and effectiveness of fertility regulation methods. Its second was to study the behavioral and social determinants of fertility regulation. Some of these studies have focused on "the relative safety

---

[460] A34/3, *supra* note 250, at 32 §101.
[461] A33/9, *supra* note 139, at 22 § 10.
[462] A40/3, *supra* note 311, at 90 § 87.
[463] *Id.* at § 127.
[464] EB81/22, *supra* note 176, at 3.

of different methods of female sterilization, the sequelae of induced abortions, and the possible sequelae of vasectomy:"[465] Other studies had focused on "the various factors affecting the choice and continuation of use of different methods of fertility regulation in developing countries, and the community barriers that impede access to family planning:"[466]

The second axis was devoted to the development of new methods. Six *Task forces* were conducting research on systemic long-acting agents, post-ovulatory methods, vaccines, male fertility regulation methods, natural methods, and the use of plants. They had conducted large-scale clinical trials (180 international multi-center trials involving more than 185,000 subjects in 150 centers in 53 countries).[467] As for natural methods, while the effectiveness of the method was considered good, its application was considered improbable. However, a training manual entitled "Family fertility education" had been developed and disseminated.[468]

Finally, the third axis was devoted to the prevention and management of infertility.[469]

These elements were also reported in 1988 in the biannual report of the HRP[470] and in the Director-General's report on WHO activities.[471]

It should be noted, however, that since the Special Programme was intended only for the rapid improvement of existing methods of fertility regulation and the development of new methods, other activities in the

---

465 *Id.* at 4.
466 *Id.*
467 *Id.* at 5.
468 *Id.* at 7.
469 *Id.*
470 World Health Organization [WHO], *Research in Human Reproduction, Biennial Report 1986-1987,* (1988), https://apps.who.int/iris/handle/10665/42106.
471 World Health Organization [WHO], A42/3, *Report of the Director-General on the work of WHO in 1988, in* 42d World Health Assembly, Geneva, 8-13 May 1989, Part I: Resolutions and Decisions, Annex 7 at 168-69 (1989), https://apps.who.int/iris/handle/10665/171211?locale-attribute=fr&.

field of human reproduction remained the responsibility of the general WHO reproductive programme (scientific and technical advice, provision of equipment, payment of personnel, research training grants, etc.) with the support of UNFPA. This included support for the establishment of research institutions in the context of national family planning programs, research projects on factors influencing acceptance of family planning services, and studies on the side effects of contraceptive agents. Such activities had taken place in 1972 in Egypt (including studies on the metabolic effects of oral contraceptives, female sterilization, and early pregnancy termination), Iran, and Pakistan. Also in 1972, a WHO research team on the methodology of clinical trials of fertility regulation agents was established in Bangkok.[472] In 1994, HRP confirmed this idea by pointing out that the *Division of Family Health* was active in reproductive health in addition to the Programme. Indeed, the Programme could not be involved in all areas of research because of its limited resources.[473]

Training, research dissemination and collaboration

Research training

In 1971, following the work of the *Human Reproduction Unit*, WHO continued to expand its education and training programs. It also continued to provide advisory services to Member States in the field of family planning.[474] In 1972, the Regional Director for the WHO Western Pacific Regional Committee reported that two courses on the health aspects of family planning were held in Manila and attended by WHO staff and observers from FAO, UNESCO, and UNICEF. Training workshops on this topic had also been held in China (Taiwan) and Malaysia (Kuala Lumpur).[475]

---

[472] *Work of WHO 1972, supra* note 242.
[473] *Challenges, Biennial Report: 1992-1993, supra* note 312, at 6.
[474] *Work of WHO 1971, supra* note 123, at 132-36 § 8.29.
[475] WHO & Reg'l Comm. W. Pac., WPR/RC23/3,*Twenty-second Annual Report of the Regional Director to the Regional Committee for the Western Pacific Covering the Period, 1*

In 1972, the *Advisory Group* recommended that a task force be established to address the lack of trained fertility regulation personnel.[476] From October 30 to November 1, 1972, a consultation was then held in Geneva to discuss research training. It was agreed that training should be increased in areas where gaps existed, particularly in reproductive biology, synthesis of new compounds, product development, pharmacology, toxicity testing, clinical trials, and monitoring of products in use, especially for side effects. A WHO staff member was to be appointed to undertake the full development of this aspect of the Expanded Programme. Twenty-four investigator exchange and research training grants were awarded to scientists from 12 countries and a seminar on clinical trial methodology was held in Bangkok in April 1973 with the participation of staff from the *Clinical Research Centres* in Bombay, Seoul, Manila, Bangkok, and Chandigarh. Other seminars, workshops, and publications were also held under the auspices of the WHO Expanded Programme.[477]

In 1980, the Director-General emphasized strengthening human reproductive research at the national level within the framework of the Special Programme, particularly in developing countries. In his eyes, this should be done through the training of research personnel, the strengthening of institutions, and the establishment and development of collaborating centers.[478] Seven years later, the Director-General concluded that these objectives had been achieved.[479]

Collaboration and cooperation

According to the Director-General, "the Special Programme is the main instrument within the United Nations system for conducting, promoting, evaluating and coordinating international research on

---

July 1971 - 30 June 1972, at 45-46 (1972), https://apps.who.int/iris/handle/10665/355243?search-result=true&query=WPR%2FRC23%2F3&scope=&rpp=10&sort_by=score&order=desc.

476 HR/72.5a, *supra* note 134, at 31.

477 *HR/73.5a*, *supra* note 245, at 34.

478 A33/9, *supra* note 139, at 15 §63.

479 A40/3, *supra* note 311, at 98 § 128.

human reproduction, fertility regulation, and family planning. All activities are oriented towards the needs of developing countries."[480] To this end, the Programme collaborates with intergovernmental and non-governmental organizations as well as with national and private institutions.

In 1971, WHO presented a project related to the Special Programme on Family Planning with a focus on maternity.[481] In this project, WHO collaborated with other organizations, including UNICEF, UNFPA, the *Population Council*, and USAID.[482] The World Bank and UNFPA also provided support to WHO for large-scale national family planning programmes.[483] Collaboration between WHO and the Government of Thailand had also taken place on an interregional research project to evaluate fertility control agents.[484] In 1972, the Director-General revealed that agreements had been reached with three pharmaceutical companies and *Clinical Research Centres* to conduct trials on new agents and to allow WHO to obtain a number of rights to the products or devices tested. He also reported that work had been done to provide equipment (spare parts and reagents) to research institutions to support them.[485]

In 1980, the program also continued to coordinate its activities with other organizations.[486] It coordinated research activities in 82 countries, including 55 developing countries.[487] That same year, the Health Assembly also asked the CEO to work on "increase extrabudgetary support for health research that is coordinated or sponsored by

---

[480] EB81/22, *supra* note 176, at 3.
[481] HR/71.4 add. 1, *supra* note 145, at 25.
[482] *Id.* at 26.
[483] *Id.* at 31.
[484] *Id.* at 140-144.
[485] *Work of WHO 1972*, *supra* note 242.
[486] A33/9, *supra* note 139, at 22 §13.
[487] A34/3, *supra* note 250, at §§56, 101-105.

WHO."[488] Thus, in 1981, the Director-General cited the Special Programme as an example of the mutual strengthening of WHO's research and technical cooperation: "the management of research is carried out on a cooperative basis, and the research itself - for instance, research carried out on intrauterine contraceptive devices - is pursued on a collaborative basis, both "horizontal" (institutions of different countries working together) and "vertical" (scientists in various countries attacking different aspects of a common problem, in accordance with a defined strategy)."[489]

In 1987, the programme was devoting one-third of its budget (about $7 million[490]) to expanding and improving the capacity for research in developing countries. At the inception of the Programme, a global network of *Clinical Research Centres,* mainly located in developing countries (80%), had been established to conduct clinical trials.[491] In order to promote national research on human reproduction, work was also done to strengthen research institutions in these countries. This was the case, for example, in China with 13 million dollars, about half of which came from UNFPA, or in Kenya with 3.5 million dollars, or in India and Indonesia. With the same logic, various grants were awarded for a value of 13 million dollars, including research training grants for 980 scientists from 60 countries. 130 major scientific meetings, organized by the Programme, were also held in some 40 countries (35 seminars, 56 workshops and 39 symposia) and 125 training courses were organized. The Special Programme had also provided equipment and reagents for $33 million (16% of the total resources of the Special Programme since its inception) to support laboratories. Overall, the studies supported by the Programme had been cited in more than 6,000

---

[488] WHO Res. WHA33.25, *On Development and Coordination of Biomedical and Health Services Research,* (May 23, 1980), *in* 33d World Health Assembly, Geneva, 5-23 May 1980, resolutions and decisions, at 25-26 (1980), https://apps.who.int/iris/handle/10665/155550?search-result=true&query=WHA33.25&scope=&rpp=10&sort_by=score&order=desc.

[489] A34/3, *supra* note 250, at 14 §56.

[490] EB81/22, *supra* note 176, at 11. Based on an expenditure commitment of approximately $21 million in 1987.

[491] *Id.* at 7-8.

publications.[492] The HRP also collaborated with different organizations. These collaborations, particularly with the pharmaceutical industry, had enabled the HRP to conduct trials on more than 60 drugs and equipment. The HRP also continued to serve as an advisory body on family planning to ministries of health, national and international organizations and institutions upon request.[493]

In 1988, the Director-General stated that work to strengthen research at the national level, particularly in developing countries, had also continued, as had the work of scientific and technical cooperation between developed and developing countries.[494] In 1990, an HRP report highlighted the program's long-term institutional development grant. This grant, which had benefited 38 institutions since 1986, was seen as the main instrument for building research capacity at the national level and for strengthening the physical and human resources of institutions. This support was also provided through research training grants that had benefited 1,122 scientists from 357 institutions.[495] In 1993, the Director-General also referred to the relationship between UNFPA and WHO to strengthen national research capacities.[496]

In 2006, the HRP was working with a network of more than 120 institutions in 59 developing countries on its research activities. 53 of these institutions had been officially designated as WHO Collaborating Centres in early 2004.[497] The programme provided financial and

---

[492] *Id.* at 8.

[493] *Id.* at 9.

[494] WHO A42/3, *Report of the Director-General on the work of WHO in 1988, in* 42d World Health Assembly, Geneva, 8-13 May 1989, Part I: Resolutions and Decisions, Annex 7 at 168-69 §§ 79-80 (1989), https://apps.who.int/iris/handle/10665/171211?locale-attribute=fr&.

[495] *Biennial Report 1988-1989, supra* note 185, at 12.

[496] WHO A46/3, *Report of the Director-General on the work of WHO,* (Apr. 7, 1993), *in* 46th World Health Assembly, Geneva, 3-14 May 1993, Resolutions and Decisions, annex 13 at 168-69 § 71 (1993), https://apps.who.int/iris/handle/10665/176262?locale-attribute=ru&.

[497] World Health Organization [WHO], *Sexual and Reproductive Health: Laying the Foundation for a more just World through Research and Action, Biennial Report 2004-2005,* at 43 (2006), https://apps.who.int/iris/handle/10665/43497.

technical support to enable them to develop their capacity in their country.[498] In 2009, there were only 44 such centers, but they were joined by the *Guttmacher Institute* in New York.[499] To give concrete examples of cooperation, between 2008 and 2009, WHO collaborated in the Americas with the *Centro Latinoamericano de Perinatologia/Salud de la Mujer y Reproductiva* (CLAP/SMR) and UNFPA for the dissemination and implementation of reproductive health guidelines and tools. 5,000 copies of Spanish-language family planning manuals[500] were distributed in 16 of the 18 Spanish-speaking countries in Latin America. A training workshop on these manuals was also held in September 2009 for English-speaking Caribbean countries. During the same period, in Southeast Asia and the Western Pacific, 25 research capacity-building grants were awarded to institutions in the region.[501] In Eastern Europe and Central Asian Republics, the UNFPA-WHO Strategic Partnership Programme (SPP) supported the implementation in Kyrgyzstan, Tajikistan, Turkmenistan, and Uzbekistan of the introduction of WHO guidelines on integrating family planning and the management of sexually transmitted infections into primary health care.[502] The HRP also continued its work with a series of six regional and subregional capacity-building workshops involving 39 countries from the African, Southeast Asian, and Western Pacific regions. These workshops were conducted within the framework of the UNFPA-WHO Strategic Partnership Programme (SPP) on Capacity Building in Research and Program Development.[503] The main objective was to help countries improve the quality of services and achieve universal access to reproductive health and to introduce them to the full range of

---

[498] *Biennial Report 2002-2003, supra* note 9.

[499] *HRP 2008-2009, supra* note 186, at 19.

[500] These manuals included the Decision Making Tool for family planning clients and providers (DMT) and the Global handbook for family planning providers.

[501] *HRP 2008-2009, supra* note 186, at 23.

[502] *Id.* at 26.

[503] *Id.* at 19.

guidelines on family planning, sexually transmitted infections, and maternal and newborn health.[504]

In 2009, collaboration with developing countries to strengthen their national research capacity remained a central objective of HRP. One-third of HRP's operating budget was targeted toward this goal (about $6 million[505]), through two main types of grants. First, long-term institutional development grants renewable for up to 10 years that provide technical support including training, equipment, expert advice, and other resources to support a research program consistent with country needs. Second, research training grants for scientists from developing countries to enable them to train at an institution other than their own. There were also grants for resource maintenance, courses, workshops, seminars, and promotion of best practices through centers of excellence.[506] In 2008 and 2012, strengthening HRP's in-country research capacity was also a focus through support to national and regional research. This was done through the provision of various grants, in particular Long Term Institutional Development (LID) grants to institutions to develop research infrastructure. Institutions receiving these grants were also monitored and were eligible for further grants to maintain their achievements. The HRP funded and collaborated with 103 research centers in 55 countries around the world (11 in the Americas, 10 in Europe, 23 in Africa and the Eastern Mediterranean, and 11 in Southeast Asia and the Western Pacific).[507] This support from the HRP had led to an increase in the high quality scientific output of the collaborating centers, published in peer-reviewed journals.[508] In 2014, HRP had continued in this vein by awarding 12 long-term institutional development grants and 21 individual research training

---

[504] *Id.* at 20.

[505] World Health Organization [WHO], HRP/PCC(23)/2010/8, *Financial Report 2008-2009, in* 23d meeting Policy and Coordination Committee (PCC), at 6 (2010) https://cdn.who.int/media/docs/default-source/hrp/hrp-financial-rpt2008-2009.pdf?sfvrsn=b887d7c7_2.

[506] World Health Organization [WHO], *Review of Global Work of WHO on Health Research: HRP*, at 3 (2009), https://apps.who.int/iris/handle/10665/127184.

[507] *External Evaluation 2008-2012, supra* note 1, at 30.

[508] *Id.* at 31

grants. HRP had also joined *ESSENCE on Health Research (Enhancing Support for Strengthening the Effectiveness of National Capacity Efforts),* which is a network to improve coordination and alignment of investments in research capacity building.[509] Similarly, in 2015, HRP had awarded long-term institutional development (LID) grants to 10 institutions and research training grants to 13 individuals.[510]

A 2017 report indicates that the programme supported the WHO Regional Office for Africa in publishing a guide on best practices in family planning programs.[511] In 2018, HRP also worked with the *Johns Hopkins Bloomberg School of Public Health* to write *Family Planning: a Global Handbook for Providers*[512] which aimed to translate scientific evidence about key contraceptive methods into practical advice. This project notably included a new section "on how family planning providers can respect, protect, and fulfil the human rights of their clients."[513] Finally, regarding adolescent sexual and reproductive health, HRP worked with Family Planning 2020 (FP2020) to provide support to more than 25 countries to include improving adolescent access to contraception in their national plans. FP2020 is a "global movement that works towards enabling 120 million more women and girls to use contraceptives by 2020."[514]

Over the course of its history, HRP's mission has evolved from generating evidence to defining and supporting the implementation of standards. This has led to greater cooperation between HRP and PDRH. This cooperation can be seen, for example, in the *Implementing Best Practices Initiative - IBP Network,* a global network supporting the

---

[509] *Highlights of 2014, supra* note 329, at 15.
[510] *HRP Highlights of 2015, supra* note 385, at 18.
[511] World Health Organization [WHO], *HRP Annual Report 2017,* at 4 (2018), https://apps.who.int/iris/handle/10665/260493.
[512] World Health Organization [WHO], *Family Planning - A Global Handbook for Providers,* (May 31, 2018) https://www.who.int/publications/i/item/9780999203705.
[513] World Health Organization [WHO], *HRP Annual Report 2018,* at 6 (2019), https://apps.who.int/iris/handle/10665/310956.
[514] *Id.* at 32.

implementation of family planning.[515] The *IBP Network* has been hosted by WHO since 2000 and the HRP provides the secretariat.[516] This family planning and reproductive health network has 85 member organizations including NGOs and universities. The *IBP Network* works to disseminate HRP research, WHO guidelines, and USAID's *High Impact Practices* on family planning and reproductive health to the world.[517] In 2009, PBI partners also supported the *Bill and Melinda Gates Institute for Population and Reproductive Health* to plan and organize the International Conference on Family Planning: Research and Best Practices in Kampala, Uganda, which was attended by more than 1,300 policymakers, researchers, and health professionals from 61 countries.[518] As another example of its work, during 2017, PBI had conducted 15 webinars on the WHO reproductive health guidelines, reaching over 1,000 participants from 45 countries.[519]

Beginning in 2013, HRP's goal was to build strong regional networks of reproductive health research, training, and mentoring centres, as envisioned by the *HRP Alliance* to move from research to implementation.[520] However, it appears that one evaluation report[521] considers that this process of creating a regional network through the *HRP Alliance* was launched without an explicit strategy and with insufficient allocation of human resources leading to slow progress.[522] The same report specifies four objectives for the *HRP Alliance*. First, strengthening the research capacity of institutions in low-resource settings. Second, promoting research capacity building in priority areas of sexual and reproductive health research at the global and regional

[515] *HRP 2013-2017, supra* note 4, at 52.
[516] World Health Organization [WHO], *HRP Annual Report 2017*, (2018), https://apps.who.int/iris/handle/10665/260493.
[517] *HRP Annual Report 2020, supra* note 8, at 53.
[518] World Health Organization [WHO], *HRP Highlights 2009*, at 5 (2010), https://apps.who.int/iris/handle/10665/70347.
[519] World Health Organization [WHO], *HRP Annual Report 2017*, at 4 (2018), https://apps.who.int/iris/handle/10665/260493.
[520] *HRP 2013-2017, supra* note 4, at III.
[521] *Id.*
[522] *Id.* at VI-VII.

levels. Third, supporting research capacity building by implementing the core values of the *HRP Alliance* (promoting gender equality, human rights, and equitable outcomes by prioritizing investments in resource-poor settings). Fourth, monitoring and evaluating research capacity building activities.[523]

According to a 2020 report, the *HRP Alliance*'s role is to "brings together national and regional government and nongovernmental institutions conducting research in SRHR in collaboration with WHO regional and country offices, WHO country collaborators, and other HRP research partners. The Alliance currently has seven regional hubs serving the following regions: Africa (French and English-speaking), Americas, Eastern Mediterranean, South-East Asia and the Western Pacific." These include short courses on research methodology, data analysis, and skill building in scientific writing and publication procedures. By 2020, sixty-two publications on sexual and reproductive health had been published by the seven *HRP Alliance* centres.[524]

Research dissemination, advocacy and communication

In 1972, WHO continued the collaboration with the *Karolinska Institute* and the Expanded Programme of the *Human Reproduction Unit*, in particular to organize symposia on research methods applicable to reproductive endocrinology. In May 1972, a symposium was held in Stockholm with Dr. Diczfalusy on methods of studying gene transcription in reproductive cells.[525] In 1973, in order to publicize the work of the *Task Forces* to the scientific community, an article was written for the WHO Chronicle, the *Population Council*'s journal Contraception,[526] and the *International Planned Parenthood Federation*'s

---

[523] *Id.* at 23.
[524] *HRP Annual Report 2020, supra* note 8, at 4.
[525] *Work of WHO 1972, supra* note 242.
[526] *HR/73.5a, supra* note 245, at 35.

Medical Bulletin. This article was also intended to advertise for scientists to join the *Task Forces.*[527]

In 1978, the Special Programme held seminars to share information from its research. These seminars focused not only on advances in fertility regulation research, "but also specific topics such as infertility, birth control vaccines, and the safety of oral contraceptives."[528] In 1980, the Director-General reported more specifically that this dissemination was achieved through the publication of one thousand scientific articles during the first five years of operation and another thousand during 1978-1979. Seminars were also organized in developing countries, mainly on recent advances in research on fertility regulation in general and also more specifically on contraceptive vaccines, among other things. The impact of this dissemination of knowledge was significant, as pharmaceutical regulatory agencies increasingly based their decisions on the results of the research conducted under the Programme.[529] In 1980, the Health Assembly also asked the Executive Director to improve mechanisms for disseminating information on biomedical and health services research.[530]

The Special Programme also communicated through the publication of an annual report until 1985 and then, starting in 1987, through a bi-annual report. It also published a quarterly newsletter called *Progress.*[531] In 1990, the programme kept advising member-States on technical questions and also contributed heavily to the establishment of rules and the elaboration and the promotion of guidelines guarantying "that

---

[527] *Id.* at 27.

[528] World Health Organization [WHO], EB65/20, *Development and Coordination of Biomedical and Health Services Research: Report by the Director-General,* § 37 (1979), https://apps.who.int/iris/handle/10665/154398?search-result=true&query=EB65%2F20&scope=&rpp=10&sort_by=score&order=desc.

[529] A33/9, *supra* note 139, at 22 § 9.

[530] World Health Organization [WHO], Res. WHA33.25, *On Development and Coordination of Biomedical and Health Services Research,* (May 23, 1980), *in* 33d World Health Assembly, Geneva, 5-23 May 1980, resolutions and decisions, at 25-26 (1980), https://apps.who.int/iris/handle/10665/155550?search-result=true&query=WHA33.25&scope=&rpp=10&sort_by=score&order=desc.

[531] EB81/22, *supra* note 176, at 9.

sound, rational, and ethically acceptable approaches are employed in research and development of new methods of fertility regulation and in their subsequent introduction and use in health care systems."[532]

Since 1972, the HRP has produced and disseminated numerous family planning tools and guidelines. In 2008, the WHO Reproductive Health Library included 137 reviews from the *Cochrane* organization (which specializes in producing and organizing information about medical research) and instructional videos such as "no scalpel vasectomy". That year, it also appears that nearly 1,640,000 documents were downloaded from the Department's website (264,000 more than in 2007), in particular thanks to the greater availability of publications in languages other than English.[533] During the 2006-2007 biennium, for communication purposes, the HRP was also involved in a contemporary art project called "Art for Health" to raise awareness of sexual and reproductive health issues around the world.[534] Between 2008 and 2009, the HRP also continued its advocacy and information work with policymakers, researchers, and the general public. As a result, 162 information materials were produced and widely distributed, including 4 in Arabic, 4 in Chinese, 16 in French, 13 in Spanish and 8 in Russian. In 2009, the HRP also updated its website[535] and a new site was created.[536] Its content had been made available on CD-ROM for the public without a good Internet connection.[537] In terms of advocacy, the department aimed "to promote uptake of its evidence-based outputs, to build awareness of key issues in sexual and reproductive health, and to raise funds and to ensure the continued commitment and engagement of Member States, WHO and other agencies".[538] To this end, 42 new English-language technical

---

[532] *Biennial Report 1988-1989*, *supra* note 185, at 5.

[533] World Health Organization [WHO], *HRP Highlights of 2008*, at 4 (2009), https://apps.who.int/iris/handle/10665/70062.

[534] *Biennial Report 2006-2007*, *supra* note 10.

[535] This updated website is found at www.who.int/reproductivehealth.

[536] The new website is found at www.who.int/hrp.

[537] *HRP 2008-2009*, *supra* note 186, at 37.

[538] World Health Organization [WHO], *Highlights of 2011*, at 29 (2012), https://apps.who.int/iris/handle/10665/70928.

publications were produced and distributed in 2011, and fourteen were translated into official languages. That year, the department's websites were visited 2.9 million times, and 696,000 documents were downloaded.[539]

In 2014, a new communication strategy for the department had been developed. It aimed to focus communication on the events most central to the department's work. On the internet, the department's "Reproductive Health" webpage had been viewed 2 million times and the WHO Reproductive Health Library website 2.8 million times. The HRP's YouTube channel had 239,000 views (a figure that seems inconsistent with the number of views on their channel). A Twitter page (@HRPresearch) was also opened. Finally, the HRP has published 123 peer-reviewed articles in the scientific press.[540] In 2015, at conferences, the department distributed 4,000 flash drives containing more than 120 publications in multiple languages. The HRP also published 203 peer-reviewed articles in the scientific press. On the internet, the department saw an increase in the number of page views and hits compared to 2014 and an online tool[541] was also launched to search for WHO guidelines related to sexual and reproductive health.[542] That same year, the department published 25 scientific articles on family planning and contraception.[543] In June 2017, in an effort to prevent unsafe abortions, HRP, WHO, and the United Nations Department of Economic and Social Affairs launched a new, open-access database of abortion-related laws, policies, and health standards in countries around the world with the goal of enabling greater transparency and "improve countries' accountability for the protection of women's and girls' health and human rights."[544]

---

[539] *Id.* at 33.

[540] *Highlights of 2014, supra* note 329, at 16.

[541] This online tool is found at http://search.srhr.org/.

[542] *HRP Highlights of 2015, supra* note 385, at 16.

[543] *Id.* at 3.

[544] World Health Organization [WHO], *HRP Annual Report 2017,* at 11 (2018), https://apps.who.int/iris/handle/10665/260493.

Since its creation, the HRP has published several guides, such as the *WHO Medical eligibility criteria for contraceptive use* (4th edition) ("MEC") in 2010 and updated in 2015.[545] In 2013, WHO also issued guidance on *Ensuring human rights in the provision of contraceptive information and services*[546] to provide guidance for the implementation of family planning programs. In 2011, HRP also updated its *Family planning - a global handbook for providers.*[547] For example, according to an evaluation report of HRP's activities between 2008 and 2012[548], HRP is recognized in the norms, guidelines, and standards it publishes. Over the past five years, the Programme has produced 86 such documents, including 16 clinical guidelines, 51 programmatic and policy documents, and 19 position papers. The report also notes that the HRP, in collaboration with its partners, is enabling the standardization of SRH terminology and contributing to the *WHO Model List of Essential Medicines.*[549] In 2016, HRP also published the third edition of *Selected practice recommendations for contraceptive use*[550] for decision-makers and the scientific community. It has also updated its recommendations on hormonal contraceptive use in relation to HIV.[551] In 2018, the programme updated its *Family planning: a global handbook for providers*[552] which aims to translate scientific data on the main contraceptive methods into practical advice. HRP also launched an app to help family planning providers

---

[545] WHO Guidelines Rev. Comm., *Medical Eligibility Criteria for Contraceptive Use,* (Feb. 3, 2015), https://www.who.int/publications/i/item/9789241549158.

[546] WHO Guidelines Rev. Comm., *Ensuring Human Rights in the Provision of Contraceptive Information and Services,* (June 1, 2014) https://www.who.int/publications/i/item/9789241506748.

[547] World Health Organization [WHO], *Family Planning - a Global Handbook for Providers,* (2012) https://fphandbook.org/sites/default/files/hb_english_2012.pdf.

[548] *External Evaluation 2008-2012, supra* note 1.

[549] *Id.* at 10.

[550] World Health Organization [WHO], *Selected Practice Recommendations for Contraceptive Use,* (3d ed., 2016) https://www.who.int/publications/i/item/9789241565400.

[551] *Annual Report 2016, supra* note 7, at 6-7.

[552] World Health Organization [WHO], *Family Planning - A Global Handbook for Providers,* (2018), https://www.who.int/publications/i/item/9780999203705.

"recommend safe, effective and acceptable contraceptive methods."[553] In 2019, HRP said it was pleased with its *Family planning: a global handbook for providers* associated to *Training resource for family planning*[554] which aimed to develop "tools for trainers to design, implement and evaluate family planning and reproductive health training." In 2019, these two items had been disseminated by IBP Network to over 80 member organizations and nearly 10,000 individuals. Between 2008 and 2013, HRP produced 477 documents (clinical guidelines, program and policy documents, policy briefs, monitoring and evaluation reports, advocacy papers, and peer-reviewed articles, which are the most numerous).[555] During 2013, twenty-seven new technical publications in English were produced and twenty-three translations were published. HRP also published 98 peer-reviewed articles in the scientific press on its research findings. 22.3 million page views were also received on WHO's reproductive health websites, and the Programme's YouTube channel had 570,000 views (a figure that seems inconsistent with the total number of views on their YouTube channel today).[556]

As another example of its work, in 2019, HRP had published a study in the *BMJ Sexual & Reproductive Health*[557] to describe "the effectiveness of various counselling strategies that could help to increase uptake of modern contraception and continuation of such use by women."[558] Another study called ECHO (Evidence for Contraceptive Options and HIV Outcomes), published in *The Lancet*, showed that contraception did

---

[553] World Health Organization [WHO], *HRP Annual Report 2018*, at 6-7 (2019), https://apps.who.int/iris/handle/10665/310956.

[554] About TRP, TRAINING RESOURCE PACKAGE, (2022), https://www.fptraining.org/about (last visited July 4, 2023).

[555] *External Evaluation 2008-2012, supra* note 1, at 12.

[556] World Health Organization [WHO], *HRP Highlights of 2013*, at 14 (2014), https://apps.who.int/iris/handle/10665/112763.

[557] Francisca L. Cavallaro et al., *A systematic review of the effectiveness of counselling strategies for modern contraceptive methods: what works and what doesn't?*, BMJ SEXUAL & REPRODUCTIVE HEALTH, (Dec. 11, 2019), https://srh.bmj.com/content/familyplanning/early/2019/12/11/bmjsrh-2019-200377.full.pdf.

[558] World Health Organization [WHO], *HRP Annual Report 2019*, at 6 (2020), https://apps.who.int/iris/handle/10665/331637.

not affect HIV prevalence.[559] An evaluation report of the HRP's activities between 2013 and 2019 has been published,[560] noting that in terms of communication, the HRP has successfully implemented an effective strategy that uses its own and WHO's social media channels.[561]

---

[559] *Id.*

[560] *HRP 2013-2017, supra* note 4.

[561] *Id.* at IV.

Chapter 6
The philosophy and strategy of the HRP and WHO within the UN

HRP spearheads UN population programs

Resolution WHA32.15[562] of 1979 refers to previous resolutions on the role of WHO in the development and coordination of biomedical research and begins by noting "the progress made in strengthening national and regional research capabilities and in establishing research coordination mechanisms at regional and global levels." Among other things, it requested the Director-General to work to increase national research capacity and to ensure that WHO participated actively in the 1979 United Nations Conference on Science and Technology for Development. WHO thus participated in the preparation of this conference by publishing a document on science and technology for health promotion in developing countries.[563] It recommended to answer the various problems posed, such as "uncontrolled population growth [which] greatly increases the problems of achieving minimal health standards," [564] acting for the research and development of culturally acceptable and low-cost contraceptive procedures.[565]

---

[562] World Health Organization [WHO], Res. WHA32.15, *On Development and Coordination of Biomedical and Health Services Research*, (May 22, 1979), *in* 32d World Health Assembly, Geneva, 7-25 May 1979: resolutions and decisions, at 14-15 (1979), https://apps.who.int/iris/handle/10665/154319?search-result=true&query=WHA32.15&scope=&rpp=10&sort_by=score&order=desc.

[563] World Health Organization [WHO], A/CONF.81/BP/WHO, *Science and technology for health promotion in developing countries / prepared by the World Health Organization for the United Nations Conference on Science and Technology in Development, Vienna, 20-31 August 1979*, (1979), https://apps.who.int/iris/handle/10665/58964?search-result=true&query=A%2FCONF.81%2FBP%2FWHO&scope=&rpp=10&sort_by=score&order=desc

[564] *Id.* at 8-10.

[565] *Id.* at 34.

Resolution WHA32.15 also requested the Director-General to work to ensure that the research policies of WHO bodies are strategically oriented towards the goal of "Health for all by the year 2000." This was a goal initiated by resolution WHA32.30[566] in 1979. This strategy is detailed in a report of the Program Committee of the Executive Board in December 1980.[567] One principle considered fundamental, among others, in this strategy is the transfer of techniques, access to all forms of health technology and research, especially in human reproduction.[568]

The Population Action Plan and Population Conferences

In 1974, the Third World Population Conference was held in Bucharest. In May of that year, the World Health Assembly expressed itself on the subject in resolution WHA27.30.[569] In the latter, she welcomed the draft *World Population Plan of Action* to be discussed at the Conference. It also requested the Director-General to report to the Executive Board and the World Health Assembly on the implications for WHO of the outcome of the World Population Conference and the decisions of the Economic and Social Council and the United Nations General Assembly in this regard. The Director-General did this in his report of 5 December 1974.[570] In it, he recalled that the WHO wanted this Conference to be approached from a health perspective. The Organization had thus

---

[566] World Health Organization [WHO], Res. WHA32.30, *On Formulating Strategies for Health for All by the Year 2000,* (May 22, 1979), *in* 32d World Health Assembly, Geneva, 7-25 May 1979: resolutions and decisions, at 27-29 (1979), https://apps.who.int/iris/handle/10665/154334?search-result=true&query=WHA32.30&scope=&rpp=10&sort_by=score&order=desc.

[567] World Health Organization [WHO], EB67/13, *Health for all by the Year 2000 - Global Strategy: Report of the Programme Committee of the Executive Board,* (Dec. 8, 1980), https://apps.who.int/iris/handle/10665/156061?search-result=true&query=EB67%2F13&scope=&rpp=10&sort_by=score&order=desc.

[568] *Id.* at 34 § 16.

[569] World Health Organization [WHO], Res. WHA27.30, *On World Population Year and Conference, 1974,* (May 21, 1974), *in* 27th World Health Assembly Geneva Part. I: Resolutions and Decisions, at 13-14 (1974), https://apps.who.int/iris/handle/10665/85874.

[570] World Health Organization [WHO], EB55/43, *World Population Year and Conference 1974, Report by the Director-General,* (Dec. 5, 1974), https://apps.who.int/iris/handle/10665/148831?search-result=true&query=EB55%2F43&scope=&rpp=10&sort_by=score&order=desc [hereinafter EB55/43].

requested that the Ministers of Health of the different States participate actively (paragraph 6 of resolution WHA26.49). This was partly done. WHO contributed to the Third World Population Conference in several ways, in particular by drafting six background documents on various topics, including the following: Health and Family Planning; Health Aspects of Population Trends and Prospects; Health Trends and Prospects 1950-2000; Health and Human Rights; Deterioration of the Environment and Population; and Research on the Biomedical Aspects of Fertility Regulation and on the Operational Aspects of Family Planning Programmes. This last topic corresponds to the WHO Expanded Programme on Human Reproduction.

The Population Action Plan: Revealing a Materialist Anthropology

Of the five basic documents of the Bucharest Conference, the fifth was of particular importance to WHO. It was a draft *World Population Plan of Action* that was adopted unanimously by the governments present. This document can be seen as a great synthesis of the conclusions of the UN work in the field of population.[571] It also reveals the materialist philosophical presuppositions that are at its origin: "The principal aim of social, economic, and cultural development, of which population goals and policies are integral parts, is to improve levels of living and the quality of life of the people. Of all things in the world, people are the most precious. Man's knowledge and ability to master himself and his environment will continue to grow. Mankind's future can be made infinitely bright".[572] From its first sentences, this Plan considered that there is an interdependence between demographic situations and socio-economic development, which explains why demographic control (called here "population goals") was considered as an aspect allowing socio-economic development.[573] This helps to explain why the rate of

---

[571] Rep. of the U.N. World Population Conf., Bucharest, U.N. Doc. E/CONF.60/19 (1974), https://undocs.org/Home/Mobile?FinalSymbol=E%2FCONF.60%2F19&Language=E&DeviceType=Desktop&LangRequested=False [hereinafter E/CONF.60/1].

[572] *Id.* at 7 § 14(a).

[573] *Id.* at 3, 20.

population growth was identified by the UN Secretary-General, in his opening statement, as one of six key issues requiring immediate action.[574]

The *World Population Plan of Action* considered that "where trends of population growth, distribution, and structure are out of balance with social economic and environmental factors, they can at certain stages of development, create additional difficulties for the achievement of sustained development. Policies whose aim is to affect population trends must [...] be[] integrated with those policies in order to facilitate the solution of certain problems facing both developing and developed countries and to promote a more balanced and rational development."[575] In paragraph 69, the UN's materialist presupposition about human nature is also evident: "In planning measures to harmonize population trends and socio-economic change, human beings must be regarded not only as consumers but also as producers. The investment by nations in the health and education of their citizens contributes substantially to productivity."[576]

Although paragraph 6 defends the couple's right to decide how many children they want to have, it declares immediately afterwards that this right cannot be effective without knowledge of birth control methods and the provision of contraceptive services. The absence of such knowledge and services would, in fact, push couples to "have more children than they desire [...]." In general, the Plan calls for "individual reproductive behaviour and the needs and aspirations of society should be reconciled."[577] The "right of the couple" thus seems very relative here. The Director-General nevertheless notes[578] the right of the couple "to decide freely and responsibly the number and spacing of their children and to have the information, education, and means to do so."[579]

---

[574] EB55/43, *supra* note 570, at 3.
[575] E/CONF.60/19, *supra* note 571, at § 2.
[576] *Id.* at § 69.
[577] *Id.* at § 7.
[578] EB55/43, *supra* note 570, at 4.
[579] E/CONF.60/19, *supra* note 571, at § 14(f).

It also notes that "the family is the basic unit of society and should be protected by appropriate legislation and policy."[580]

The two main aspects of the HRP are addressed by the *World Population Plan of Action*, but without direct reference to the Programme. The first aspect is research.[581] The Plan calls for more research on "the assessment and improvement of existing and new methods of fertility regulation by means of research, including basic biological and applied research; the evaluation of the impact, both in short-term and long-term effects, of different methods of fertility regulation on ethical and cultural values and on mental and physical health."[582] The second aspect of the Expanded Programme is training and, more generally, education and information.[583] This aspect will be retained by the Director-General in his report as he notes that one of the general objectives set by the *World Population Plan of Action* was "to encourage the development and good management of appropriate education, training, research, information and family health services, as well as statistics."[584] It also cites paragraphs 71 to 80 as being of particular importance to WHO, and in particular paragraphs "78(c), 78(i), 78(j), and 78(k); these refer respectively to reduction of maternal and infant mortality, improvement of existing and new methods of fertility regulation, evaluation of the impact of different methods of family planning on health, patterns of family formation and health, and treatment of and causes of sterility." Note that paragraph 29(c) calls for "ensur[ing] that family planning, medical and related social services aim not only at the prevention of unwanted pregnancies." The Director-General also notes the call for "encourage the development and good management of […] family health services."[585] For him, paragraphs 27-43, under the heading "Reproduction, family formation, and the status of women," are also of particular importance to WHO. Finally, he considers

---

[580] *Id.* at § 14(g).
[581] *Id.* at §§ 71-80.
[582] *Id.* at § 78(i).
[583] *Id.* at §§ 81-93.
[584] EB55/43, *supra* note 570, at 3.
[585] E/CONF.60/19, *supra* note 571, at § 15(h).

important for the WHO the invitation made to the UNFPA "with the cooperation of the organizations concerned, to produce a guide for international assistance in population matters which would be made available to recipient countries."[586]

The Director-General's report was considered by the Executive Board[587] and the World Health Assembly in 1975, with resolution WHA28.44.[588] The resolution expressed satisfaction with WHO's contribution to the World Population Conference and welcomes the emphasis placed by the World Population Plan of Action on "the interrelationships of population and socioeconomic development." It also recognized "the need to improve health through support to research on all aspects of human reproduction, including methods of fertility regulation and the impact of family planning on health". Finally, it requested the Director-General "to intensify activities related to family health care [...] to participate fully in the development of activities in the sectors of the World Population Plan of Action related to health".

Seven years after the Bucharest Conference, in 1981, the UN Economic and Social Council resolution 1981/28 also called for the development and strengthening of activities to implement the *World Population Plan of Action* and specifically requested WHO to ensure that population issues are addressed in its various conferences and its regular programme of work. It also urged UNFPA, WHO, and governments "to give high priority to research on human reproduction and the development of more acceptable, safer, and more effective means of

---

586 *Id.* at § 105.

587 WHO Executive Board Res. EB55.R60, *On Coordination with Other Organizations of the United Nations System: World Population Year and Conference, 1974,* (January 31, 1975), *in* 56th session, Geneva, 20-31 January 1975, Part I: resolutions: annexes, (1975), https://apps.who.int/iris/bitstream/handle/10665/90743/EB55R60_eng.pdf?sequence=1&isAllowed=y.

588 World Health Organization [WHO], Res. WHA28.44, *On World Population Year and Conference, 1974,* (May 28, 1975), *in* 28th World Health Assembly Geneva, 13-30 May 1975, Part I Resolutions and Decisions, at 22-23 (1975), https://apps.who.int/iris/handle/10665/92942?search-result=true&query=%22WHA28.44%22&scope=%2F&rpp=10&sort_by=score&order=desc.

fertility regulation, to promote the establishment of projects in which research workers in developed and less developed countries would cooperate fully in such research and to emphasize to public and private donors the great importance of such research."[589] The Director-General reported that in 1981, UNFPA had provided financial support for the activities of the WHO Special Programme on "Family Health."[590]

Population conferences

In 1984, the Fourth International Conference on Population was held in Mexico City.[591] At this conference, most of the aspects discussed at the 1974 Bucharest Conference were reviewed and approved. The *World Population Plan of Action* was also expanded in line with research advances.[592]

In 1994, the fifth International Conference on population was held in Cairo.[593] This conference reviewed, modified and approved the definition of "reproductive health" proposed by the WHO. "During this event, a new Programme of Action[594] was adopted as a guide for national and international action in the field of population and development for twenty years. This new agenda for action has emphasized the indissoluble relationship between population and

---

[589] U.N. Economic and Social Council Res. E/RES/1981/28, *On Strengthening of Actions Concerned with the Fulfilment of the World Population Plan of Action*, §4 (May 6, 1981), https://digitallibrary.un.org/record/32816?ln=fr#record-files-collapse-header.

[590] World Health Organization [WHO], A35/17, *Collaboration with the United Nations System: General Matters: Report by the Director-General*, at 10 § 5.14 (Apr. 2, 1982), https://apps.who.int/iris/bitstream/handle/10665/156743/WHA35_17_eng.pdf?sequence=1&isAllowed=y.

[591] Rep. of the Int'l Conf. on Population, Mexico City, 6-14 August. 1984, U.N. Doc. E/CONF.76/19 (1984), https://documents-dds-ny.un.org/doc/UNDOC/GEN/N84/214/34/PDF/N8421434.pdf?OpenElement.

[592] CONFERENCES | POPULATION, UNITED NATIONS, https://www.un.org/en/conferences/population (last visited July 4, 2023).

[593] Rep. of the Int'l Conf. on Population & Dev., U.N. Doc. A/CONF.171/13/Rev.1 (1994), https://documents-dds-ny.un.org/doc/UNDOC/GEN/N95/231/26/IMG/N9523126.pdf?OpenElement.

[594] Int'l Conf. on Population & Dev., *Programme of Action*, (1994), https://www.unfpa.org/sites/default/files/event-pdf/PoA_en.pdf.

development and focuses on meeting the needs of individuals within the framework of universally recognized human rights standards rather than simply responding to demographic goals."[595] The WHO had actively participated in the organization of this conference. In his report on the subject,[596] the Director-General recalled that:

> The 1974 World Population Conference, held in Bucharest, focused on the role of development in decreasing population growth, and the emphasis in family planning programmes was on reducing fertility to this end. A decade later, the 1984 International Conference on Population held in Mexico City recognized the links between fertility regulation, health, development, and the well-being of the whole family. The Economic and Social Council, in its resolution 1991/93 on the 1994 Conference, emphasized the national sovereignty of all countries in formulating, adopting and implementing their population policies, mindful of their particular conditions, and consistent with human rights and with the responsibilities of individuals, couples and families. The challenge for the 1994 Conference was to ensure that population policies would be implemented as part of a general effort to improve the health of individuals, and to shift the focus of population policies away from a demographic perspective towards one that emphasizes the individuals quality of life.[597]

In 1998, the HRP report stated that while fertility regulation remained the Special Programme's primary area of research, it had expanded its

---

[595] CONFERENCES | POPULATION, UNITED NATIONS, https://www.un.org/en/conferences/population (last visited July 4, 2023).

[596] World Health Organization [WHO], A48/35, *Collaboration within the United Nations System: International Conference on Population and Development, 1994: Report by the Director-General,* (Mar. 14, 1995), https://apps.who.int/iris/handle/10665/177518?search-result=true&query=A48%2F35&scope=&rpp=10&sort_by=score&order=desc.

[597] *Id.* at § 2.

area of work in response to questions posed at the 1994 Conference and at the 1995 World Conference on Women.[598]

Co-sponsorship with UN organizations

The 1987 Director-General's report proposing the memorandum on the administrative structure of the Special Programme and co-sponsorship was discussed in the Commission during the forty-first World Health Assembly in 1988.[599] It was positively received by the States present (Brazil, Bulgaria, Chile, China, Cuba, Denmark, Hungary, India, Malawi, Mexico, Mozambique, Nepal, the Netherlands, the Republic of Korea, Sweden, Tunisia, Turkey, the United Kingdom, the Union of Soviet Socialist Republics, Zaire, and Zimbabwe). The Hungarian delegate placed the Programme in a context where, since the mid-1950s, world population growth had become a concern. This concern had led to suggestions to try to solve this problem. In this context, the Netherlands recalled that, faced with the rapid population growth in developing countries, its cooperation with these countries had been through the support of UNFPA, WHO and UNICEF programs aimed at providing family planning methods to these countries. The delegate from the Netherlands also stressed that, in order to be accepted by the population, these methods must be "safe and reliable," but this is not enough because "social and psychological factors also played a considerable part." The Netherlands hoped that co-sponsorship of the Programme would lead to "increased cooperation and better knowledge concerning the acceptability and applicability of various family planning methods." In the same line of thinking, Denmark also attached importance to the work of the *Task Force* on the "behavioural and social determinants of fertility regulation." Interestingly, he seemed uncomfortable with the term "fertility regulation." According

---

[598] *Biennial Report: 1996-1997, supra* note 315.
[599] World Health Organization [WHO], WHA41/1988/REC/3, *Special Programme of Research, Development and Research Training in Human Reproduction*, May 9, 1988, *in* 41st World Health Assembly, Geneva, 2-13 May 1988, at 35-43 (1988), https://apps.who.int/iris/handle/10665/164199?search-result=true&query=WHA41%2F1988%2FREC%2F3&scope=&rpp=10&sort_by=score&order=desc.

to the country delegate, this expression "failed to catch the principle and philosophy underlying the Special Programme, which was that fertility regulation was more than just a matter of numbers but was closely connected with health policy and formed an important part of the primary health care concept." This was also the view of the delegate from Cuba, who felt that this programme had made governments realize that fertility regulation is a health issue that goes beyond the strictly demographic level. It should also be noted that the Brazilian delegate wanted to ensure that research proposals were in line with national legislation and respect for ethical principles. This central coordination by governments would, in his view, be the best way to oversee proposals from non-governmental sources. The delegate from Zimbabwe called on scientists, especially those from developing countries, to use natural methods and herbs as a means of contraception.

Other delegates also spoke about the concrete situation in their countries. Thus, the delegate of India, fully supporting the Special Programme, stated that "India's family welfare programme aimed at the small-family norm, not only because of the effect of population increase on economic development but also, more importantly, from the point of view of the health of the population, and particularly of women and children." In particular, he hoped that research on the behavioral and social determinants of fertility regulation could be encouraged. He also reported that India was interested in developing new contraceptive methods, particularly injectable formulations and the development of a contraceptive vaccine. Turkey, on the other hand, was pleased with its national family planning programme aimed at reducing the population growth rate to 1.76% by the year 2000. In line with this, the country had passed the first population planning law in 1965 and legalized abortion before ten weeks. Other states also announced specific targets for population growth rates. This was the case in the Republic of Korea, where the delegate stated that family planning policies implemented since 1960 had reduced the fertility rate from 6 to 1.95 children and the annual population growth rate from 2.84

to 1.19 percent. The delegate from Nepal went further and stated that "the basic need of his country was to reduce population growth to less than 2% by the end of the century." To this end, various contraceptive methods were being used in the villages, integrating family planning into the broader health programmes. The delegate from China reported that his government was "attached great importance to family planning, considering it to be of deep significance." China "relied on three inseparable elements to implement its population growth control policy: national policies and activities, community and voluntary participation, and scientific and technological work."

In 1992, on the occasion of the 20th anniversary of the Special Programme, the three co-sponsors of the Programme were all pleased with the results achieved.[600] UNFPA Executive Director Nafis Sadik, recalling that the Fund has supported the Programme since 1974, especially welcomed the introduction of new contraceptive products and the strengthening of research capacities in biomedical and social sciences in many developing countries.[601]The UNDP Administrator, William H. Draper III, was also enthusiastic about the results of the Programme. He saw fertility control as part of every individual's right to "participate fully in community decisions and to enjoy human, economic, and political freedom."[602] Finally, World Bank President Lewis T. Preston recalled that his institution, too, had assisted the programme in an advisory capacity almost from the beginning. He felt that the HRP, through its research and research training work, had contributed to the development of a scientific consensus on the safety and effectiveness of contraceptive methods, providing "an indispensable service for the hundreds of millions of people who choose to plan their families." He considered this approach to be similar to that of the World Bank, which believed that human resource

---

[600] World Health Organization [WHO], *Reproductive Health: a Key to a Brighter Future, Biennial Report 1990-1991, Special 20th Anniversary issue,* (1992), https://apps.who.int/iris/handle/10665/38595.
[601] *Id.* at 11.
[602] *Id.* at 12.

development and poverty reduction "depend on [...] providing family planning services."[603]

WHO's strategic plans for human reproduction from 1995 onwards

In 1995, the World Health Assembly issued its resolution WHA48.10 on the role of WHO in the global strategy on human reproduction.[604] It noted the Director-General's report on maternal and child health and family planning[605] and recalled several previous resolutions on the many aspects of reproductive health.[606] The Health Assembly called on Member States to further develop and strengthen their reproductive health programmes.

In 2002, the World Health Assembly issued its resolution WHA55.19 on WHO's contribution to achieving the development goals of the Millennium Declaration.[607] In particular, it noted the goal of reducing maternal and child mortality by 2015. To achieve this goal, the WHO considered it essential to increase access to good quality primary health care information and services, including reproductive health. However, it specified that " 'primary health care services' do not include abortion except when consistent with national and, where applicable, local law, and with full respect for the various religious and ethical values and

---

603 *Id.* at 13.

604 World Health Organization [WHO], Res. WHA48.10, *On Reproductive Health: WHO's Role in the Global Strategy*, (May 12, 1995), https://apps.who.int/iris/bitstream/handle/10665/200971/WHA48_R10_fre.pdf?sequence=1&isAllowed=y

605 World Health Organization [WHO], A48/10, *Maternal and Child Health and Family Planning: Quality of Care Reproductive Health: WHO's Role in the Global Strategy, Report by the Director-General*, (Apr. 24, 1995), https://apps.who.int/iris/handle/10665/200313?search-result=true&query=A48%2F10&scope=&rpp=10&sort_by=score&order=desc.

606 Referring to WHA32.42, WHA38.22, WHA40.27, WHA41.9, WHA42.42, WHA43.10, WHA47.9 and EB95.R10. Res. WHA48.10, *supra* note 605.

607 World Health Organization [WHO], Res. WHA55.19, *On WHO's Contribution to Achievement of the Development Goals of the United Nations Millennium Declaration*, (May 18, 2002), https://apps.who.int/iris/handle/10665/78536?search-result=true&query=WHA55.19&scope=&rpp=10&sort_by=score&order=desc.

cultural backgrounds." Concerned about various situations including unsafe abortion, the resolution recalled that the WHO Constitution proclaims that one of the fundamental rights of every human being is the enjoyment of the highest attainable standard of health, and that this includes access to good quality reproductive health services, incorporating effective, affordable, and acceptable family planning services. Reaffirming resolution WHA48.10, WHO called on Member States to urgently improve access to primary health care services, including reproductive health services. It also invited the Director-General to develop a strategy to accelerate progress toward international development goals and targets related to reproductive health.

In a 2004 report, HRP Director Paul F.A. Van Look emphasized that "sexual and reproductive health problems have a broader impact on social and economic development." Thus, in the context of the Millennium Development Goals, WHO had developed a new global strategy on this issue, approved by the WHO Executive Board in January 2004 and by the World Health Assembly in May 2004. The director also noted that while contraceptive use has increased worldwide, 123 million couples, mainly in developing countries, are not using contraception, "despite wanting to space or limit the number of their children." And nearly 300 million couples were not satisfied with the methods they were using. He also noted that the HIV pandemic demonstrates the need to not only prevent "against unwanted pregnancies but also against sexually transmitted infections." To that end, he explained that the HRP was pursuing studies on the perceptions of African and Asian populations on condom use and was pursuing clinical research for the development of molecules used for medical abortions.

In 2004, the World Health Assembly issued its resolution WHA57.12 on the draft strategy on reproductive health[608] after reviewing the Director-General's document.[609] It endorsed the strategy and called on Member States to take urgent action to implement it in their national efforts. This document has been the organizational guideline for the RHR including the HRP. In general, it begins by identifying the "principal barriers to progress," specifically the inequities related to gender and poverty and the risks specific to adolescents. It then outlines a human rights-based strategy. It concludes with a reaffirmation of WHO's collaborative commitments to assist Member States.[610] In the area of reproductive health, the strategy aims to improve pregnancy, childbirth, and newborn care; provide family planning services, including infertility treatment; eliminate unsafe abortions; combat sexually transmitted infections and other gynecological conditions; and promote sexual health.

Thus, paragraph 33 guides the department to work toward accelerating progress toward international reproductive health goals. The sub-division for the promotion of family planning (FP) is guided by paragraphs 15 to 16, which deplore the lack of access to contraception in developing countries compared to developed countries as well as the high rate of people without family planning services. The subdivision for the improvement of maternal and perinatal health (MPH) is guided by paragraphs 10 to 14, which denounce the various complications, sometimes fatal for the mother or the child, related to pregnancy and childbirth that are not treated in the majority of developing countries. The subdivision for the Prevention Unsafe Abortion (PUA) is guided by paragraph 17, which denounces "unsafe abortions" (estimated at 19

---

[608] World Health Organization [WHO], Res. WHA57.12, *On Reproductive Health: Draft Strategy to Accelerate Progress towards the Attainment of International Development Goals and Targets*, (May 22, 2004), https://apps.who.int/iris/bitstream/handle/10665/20137/A57_R12-en.pdf?sequence=1&isAllowed=y.

[609] World Health Organization [WHO], *Reproductive Health Strategy to Accelerate Progress Towards the Attainment of International Development Goals and Targets*, (2004), https://apps.who.int/iris/handle/10665/68754.

[610] *Id.* at § 3.

million each year and leading to an estimated 68,000 deaths per year). The Subdivision for the Control of Sexually Transmitted and Reproductive tract infections (STI) is guided by paragraphs 18 to 22. The Subdivision of Gender, Reproductive Rights, Sexual Health and Adolescence (GRR) is guided by paragraphs 23 to 25, which address various "barriers to progress," particularly gender inequality in health care leading to lack of care and physical, sexual, and psychological violence and abuse. It is also guided by paragraph 32, which notes that laws, policies, and regulations in some countries can block or restrict access to family planning services and contraceptives. The RRM subdivision is also guided by paragraph 34, which states that the WHO strategy is based on international instruments and declarations reflecting a global consensus that relate to human rights (basic right to decide on the number of children, spacing of births, having information to do so, etc.). Finally, the GRR subdivision is guided by paragraphs 57 to 59, recommending the creation of legislative and regulatory frameworks that are conducive. One of the areas of work for this subdivision is to review laws and policies and, where necessary, modify them to support universal and equitable access to sexual and reproductive health services, education and information. Technical cooperation with countries for sexual and reproductive health (TCC) is also guided by this strategy document.

Paragraph 37 also insists on the fight against unsafe abortion, which it wants to see taken into account in the framework of the Millennium Development Goal in order to reduce the mortality associated with it. To this end, the strategy consists of strengthening and making accessible family planning services in order to avoid unwanted pregnancies and training those who perform abortions in modern techniques by providing them with the necessary drugs and equipment. The strategy also includes providing social support to women in the event of an unwanted pregnancy and, to the extent permitted by law, offering abortion services at the primary health care level and managing any complications after an unsafe abortion.[611]

These different points and paragraphs are illustrated in the figure[612] below:

Figure 1
Annotated Organizational Chart. Department of Reproductive Health and Research (RHR)including UNDP/UNFPA/WHO/World Bank Special Programme of Research, Development and Research Training in Human Reproduction (HRP)

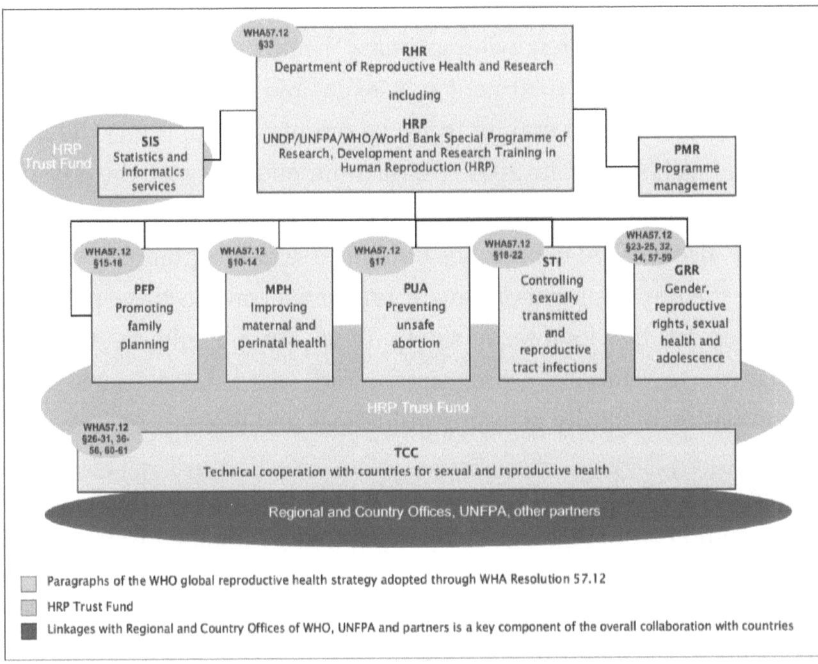

In 2008, the HRP Director reported[613] that the 62nd United Nations General Assembly in 2007 added to the Millennium Development Goals the achievement of universal access to reproductive health by 2015. He quoted former UN Secretary General Kofi Annan as saying that "The Millennium Development Goals, particularly the eradication of extreme

---

[611] World Health Organization [WHO], *Reproductive Health Strategy to Accelerate Progress Towards the Attainment of International Development Goals and Targets*, (2004), https://apps.who.int/iris/handle/10665/68754.

[612] World Health Organization [WHO], *Department of Reproductive Health and Research: Partner Brief*, at 2 (2009), https://apps.who.int/iris/handle/10665/70063.

[613] *Biennial Report 2006-2007, supra* note 10.

poverty and hunger, cannot be achieved if questions of population and reproductive health are not squarely addressed."

In 2010, WHO's strategic focus was on building health systems capacity, improving the information base for priority setting, mobilizing political will, creating supportive legislative and regulatory frameworks, and strengthening monitoring and evaluation of work. The department worked on three main themes: universal access to sexual and reproductive health, renewing primary health care, and expanding linkages between HIV treatment and sexual and reproductive health.[614] These objectives result mainly from the orientations of the WHO in its resolution WHA57.12 in 2004, the recommendations of the external evaluations of the HRP and the vision of the WHO Director-General.[615] The HRP also worked to promote and improve family planning services through the development of new or improved contraceptive methods, evaluation of the long-term safety of existing methods, technical assistance to national programs, and the development and dissemination of family planning guidelines and tools.

During 2013, a functional review of the HRP had concluded that while work should continue in the many areas covered by the Programme, it should prioritize three areas: contraception/family planning; maternal and perinatal health; and adolescent sexual and reproductive health. This review had "also recommended that each team should focus on research (biomedical, clinical, health systems, epidemiological and implementation research); guidelines, norms and standards; monitoring and evaluation; and global advocacy."[616]

---

[614] *HRP 2008-2009, supra* note 186, at 2.

[615] *Id.* at 4.

[616] World Health Organization [WHO], *HRP Highlights of 2013*, at 3 (2014), https://apps.who.int/iris/handle/10665/112763.

Chapter 7
Conclusion

It appears that the UN, through its various bodies, has been implementing a population control strategy since the 1950s. This strategy was based on the presupposition that population growth would lead to a crisis of economic development detrimental to mankind. Within the United Nations, the World Health Organization (WHO) committed to this strategy from a health perspective, believing that excessive population growth would have harmful health consequences. They thought that a smaller terrestrial population would lead to greater prosperity and better health. Scientific research was therefore launched to find technical solutions to the problem of excessive human fertility. The HRP spearheaded this research from the early 1970s onwards. Under its auspices, the main contraceptives used today were developed with this problem in mind. This work made a major contribution to the widespread use of contraception. It has even contributed to a new paradigm in which, despite initial caution from governments, contraception has become "moral". Using contraception, abortion, or sterilization has become a so-called altruistic way of serving one's own freedom and the good of the world.

It's worth noting that since 2000, research has been running out of steam. Whereas in previous years the HRP had concentrated on high-level scientific research, there's a feeling that enthusiasm waned after the massive spread of contraception worldwide. Basic biomedical research has given way to human sciences and communication. Manuals for healthcare professionals have been published, and a YouTube channel and Twitter account have been created. This can be interpreted as a need to regain a sense of purpose after the goal seems to have been achieved: no one questions contraception anymore and demographers are now predicting a demographic decline. The HRP nonetheless retains its influence, with governments interpreting its recommendations in the light of the scientific authority conferred upon it by the WHO.

Nevertheless, while the HRP was originally a body at the service of governments to meet their basic scientific research needs, its lack of orientation towards biomedical research may today be leading it to drift towards more political concerns. This concern is all the more pressing when we observe that the major American neoliberal foundations, which have a political rather than a scientific agenda, are investing heavily in the Programme. This is particularly true of the Susan Thompson Buffett Foundation, which has committed $100 million to funding the HRP in 2019.[617] From the outset, the HRP has had a close relationship with private foundations, in particular the Ford Foundation. These relationships have helped to shape the scientific research agenda. Today, these relationships are worrying insofar as they testify to a form of privatization of the Programme for political purposes, but under the seal of the WHO, which still wields considerable influence over governments.

---

[617] World Health Organization [WHO], A74/INF./4, *Voluntary contributions by Fund and by Contributor, 2019*, at 10,18 (June 29, 2020), https://www.who.int/publications/i/item/10665339657.

Appendix 1 - HRP: functioning and evolution

Expanded Programme on Human Reproduction: 1972-1986

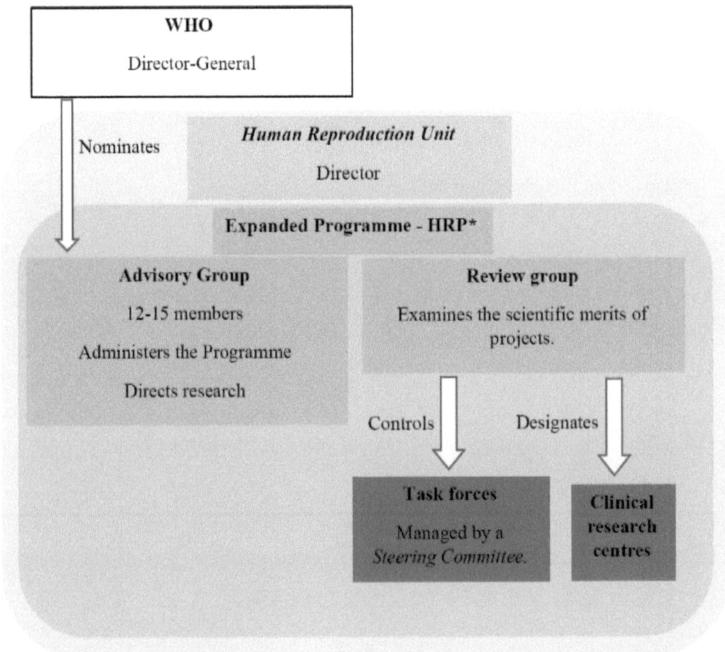

Funding: most of the programme's funding comes from voluntary contributions from member states and non-governmental organizations. In the case of the Expanded Programme, the Scandinavian countries, Canada, and the Ford and Rockefeller Foundations play a major role.

* From 1976

Special Programme on Human Reproduction: 1986-1987

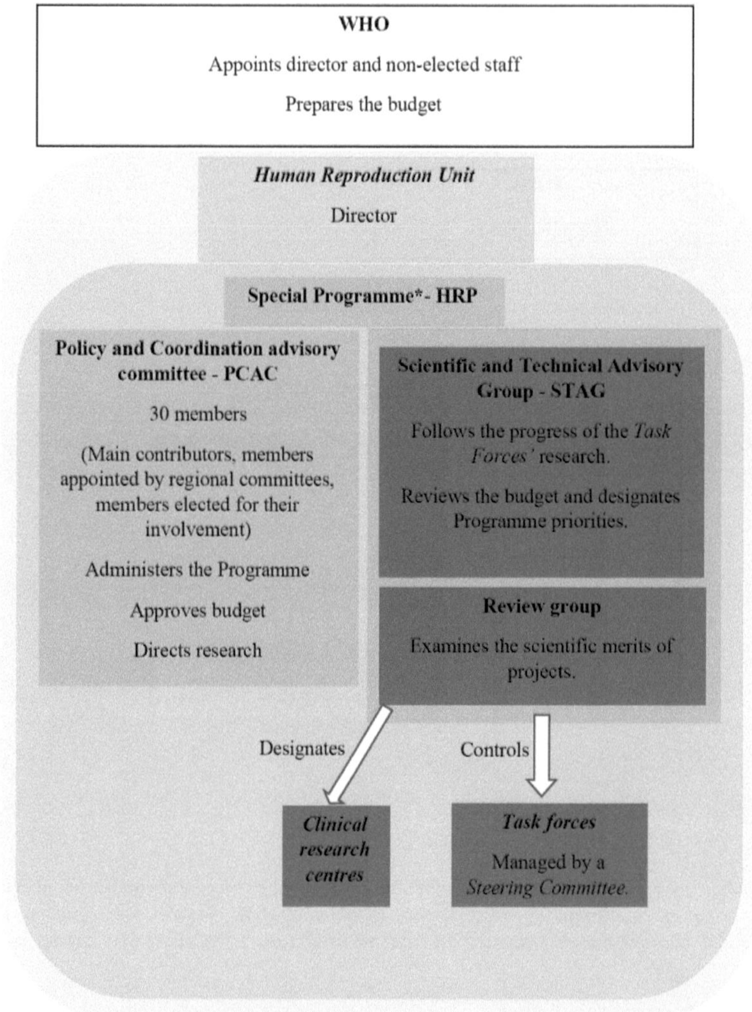

Funding: voluntary contributions from Australia, China, Cuba, Denmark, Finland, France, Germany, India, Malaysia, Mexico, Netherlands, Nigeria, Norway, Sweden, Thailand, USSR, UK, USA, Canadian International Development Research Centre, Rockefeller Foundation, UNFPA, World Bank and WHO.

*Since 1977

Special Programme on Human Reproduction: 1988-1998

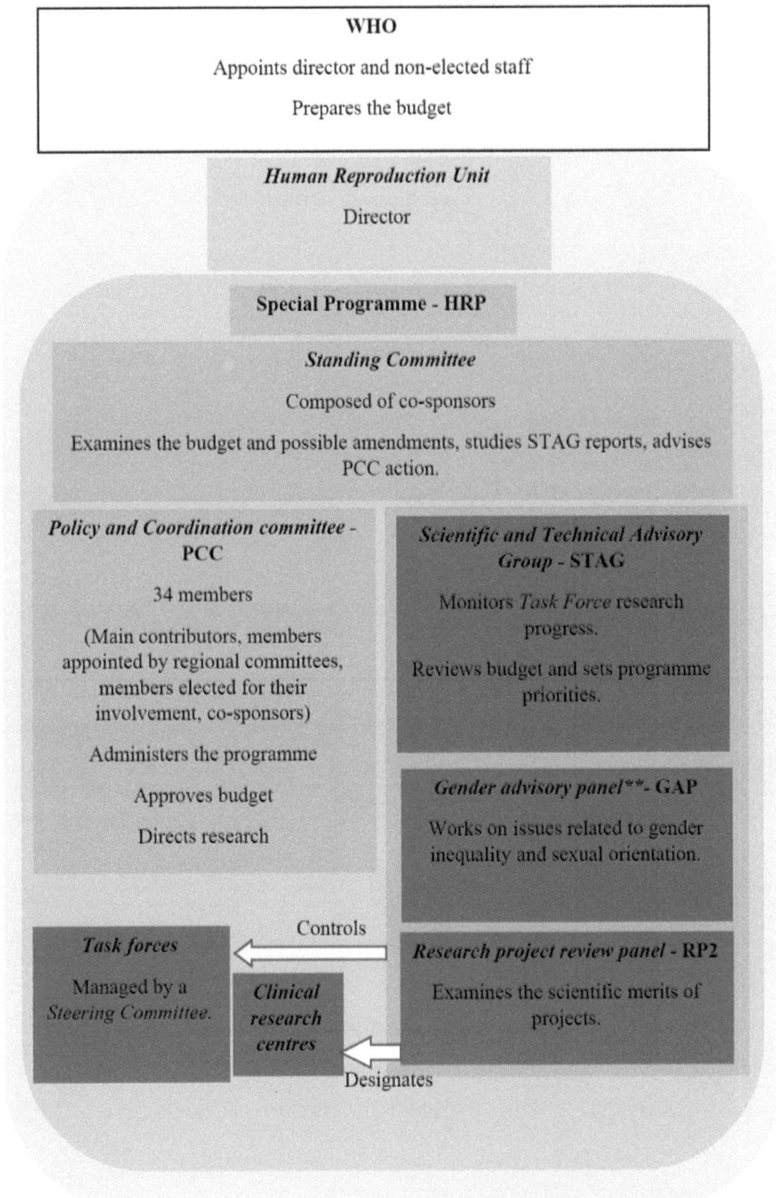

** created in 1996

Special Programme on Human Reproduction: 1998-2019

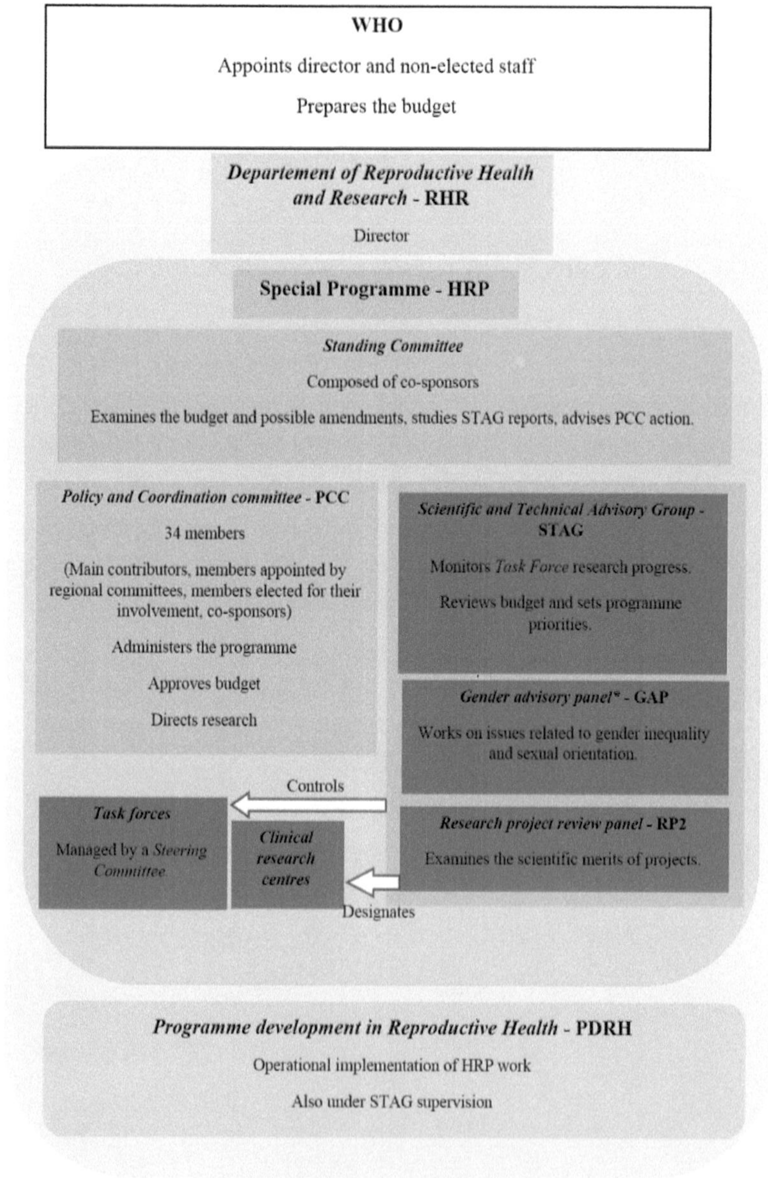

**Gender and rights advisory panel* since 2007

Special Programme on Human Reproduction: since 2019

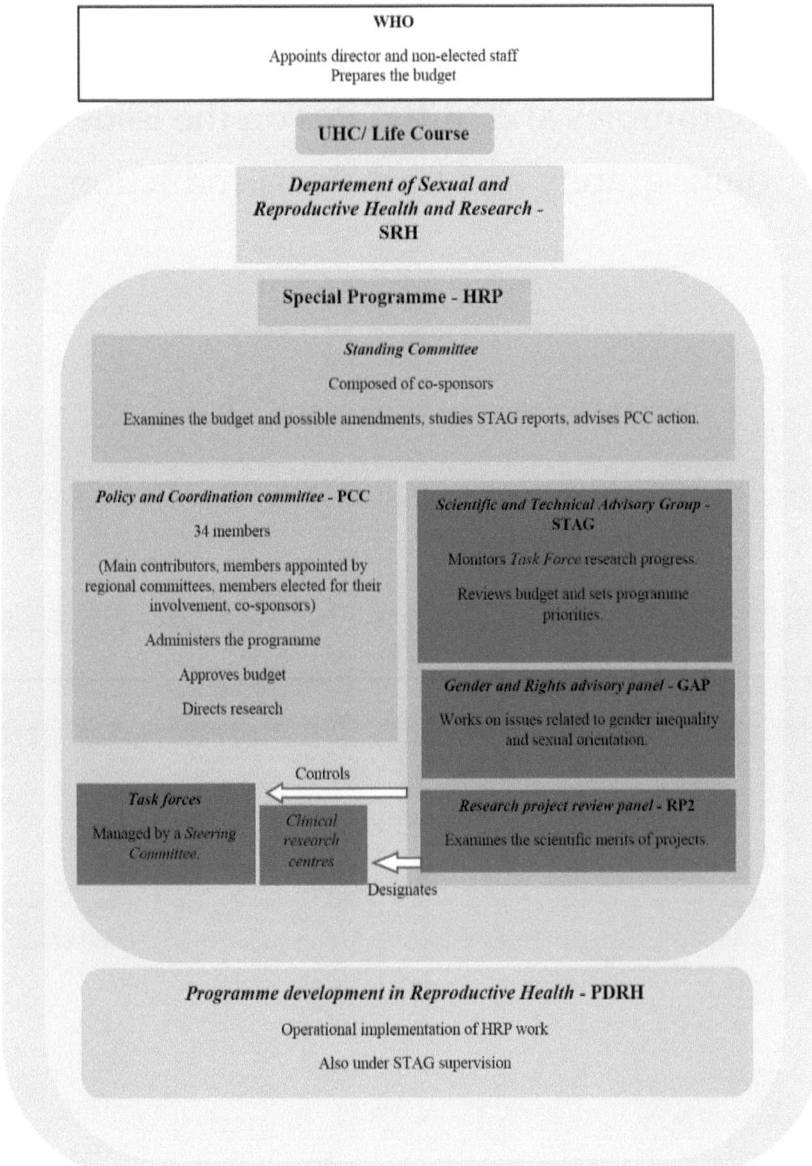

Appendix 2 - Chronological timeline showing the evolution of United Nations and WHO programmes and initiatives on the issue of demography and human reproduction.

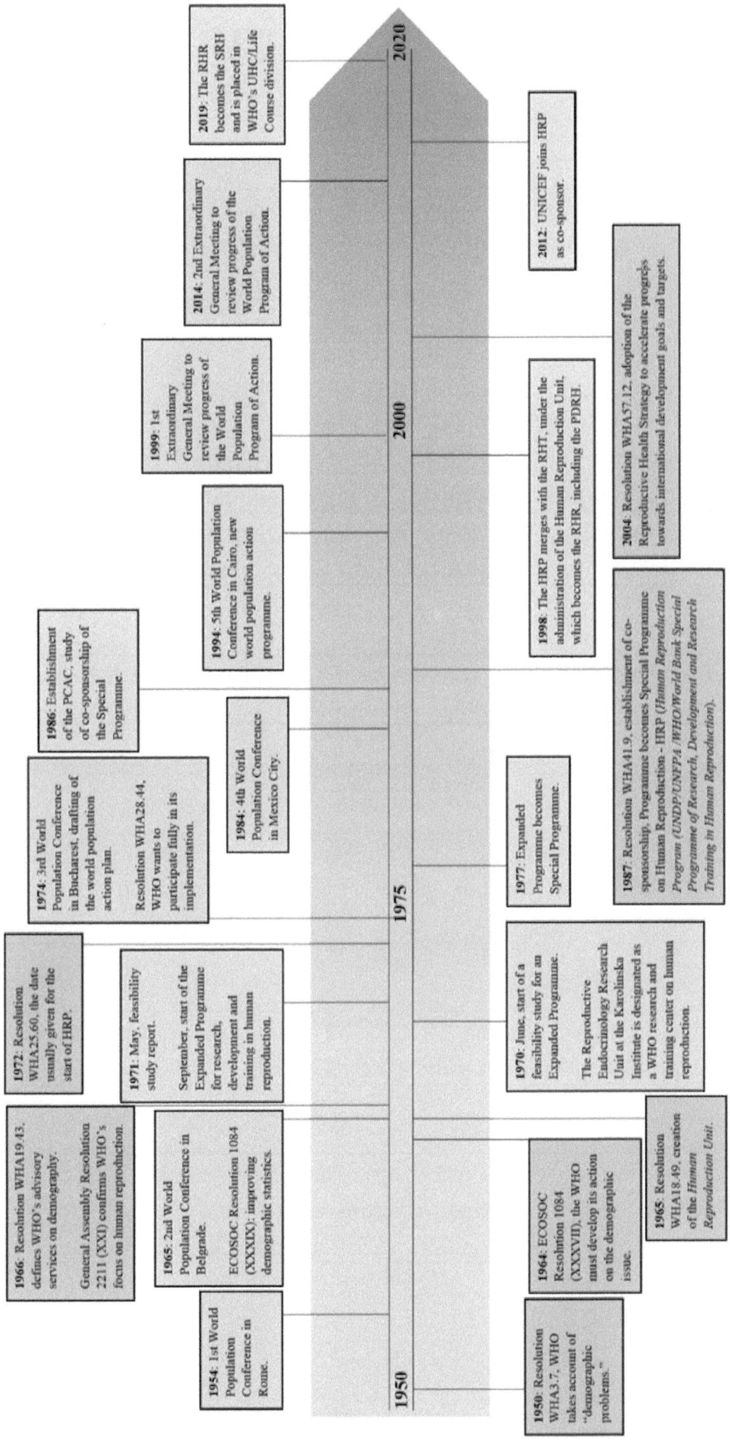
1950
1975
2000
2020
1954: 1st World Population Conference in Rome.
1966: Resolution WHA19.43, defines WHO's advisory services on demography.
General Assembly Resolution 2211 (XXI) confirms WHO's focus on human reproduction.
1965: 2nd World Population Conference in Belgrade.
ECOSOC Resolution 1084 (XXXIX): improving demographic statistics.
1972: Resolution WHA25.60, the date usually given for the start of HRP.
1971: May, feasibility study report.
September, start of the Expanded Programme for research, development and training in human reproduction.
1974: 3rd World Population Conference in Bucharest, drafting of the world population action plan.
Resolution WHA28.44, WHO wants to participate fully in its implementation.
1986: Establishment of the PCAC, study of co-sponsorship of the Special Programme.
1984: 4th World Population Conference in Mexico City.
1994: 5th World Population Conference in Cairo, new world population action programme.
1999: 1st Extraordinary General Meeting to review progress of the World Population Program of Action.
2014: 2nd Extraordinary General Meeting to review progress of the World Population Program of Action.
2019: The RHR becomes the SRH and is placed in WHO's UHC/Life Course division.
1950: Resolution WHA3.7, WHO takes account of "demographic problems."
1964: ECOSOC Resolution 1084 (XXXVII), the WHO must develop its action on the demographic issue.
1965: Resolution WHA18.49, creation of the Human Reproduction Unit.
1970: June, start of a feasibility study for an Expanded Programme.
The Reproductive Endocrinology Research Unit at the Karolinska Institute is designated as a WHO research and training center on human reproduction.
1977: Expanded Programme becomes Special Programme.
1987: Resolution WHA41.9, establishment of co-sponsorship, Programme becomes Special Programme on Human Reproduction - HRP (Human Reproduction Program (UNDP/UNFPA/WHO/World Bank Special Programme of Research, Development and Research Training in Human Reproduction).
1998: The HRP merges with the RHT, under the administration of the Human Reproduction Unit, which becomes the RHR, including the PDRH.
2004: Resolution WHA57.12, adoption of the Reproductive Health Strategy to accelerate progress towards international development goals and targets.
2012: UNICEF joins HRP as co-sponsor.

Appendix 3 – Sources

1949

World Health Organization [WHO], Res. WHA2.19, *On Co-ordination of Research, in* 2d World Health Assembly, Rome,13 June-2 July 1949, at 23 (1949), https://apps.who.int/iris/handle/10665/86082.

1950

World Health Organization [WHO], Res. WHA3.7, *On Population Problems,* (May 19, 1950), *in* 3d World Health Assembly Geneva, Part I: Resolutions and Decisions, at 17 (1950), https://apps.who.int/iris/bitstream/handle/10665/86205/WHA3.7_eng.pdf?sequence=1&isAllowed=y.
WHO, *Resolution on Population Problems,* 5th Sess. Geneva, pt. 1 at. 9 (1950), https://apps.who.int/iris/handle/10665/85604.

1951

WHO, SEA/RC4/14, *Population Problems,* Reg'l Comm. for S.E. Asia, New Delhi (1951), https://apps.who.int/iris/bitstream/handle/10665/128144/EB9_16_eng.pdf?sequence=1&isAllowed=y.

1952

WHO Executive Board, EB9/96, Pilot Study on the Voluntary Limitation of Families in India, (January 28, 1952), https://apps.who.int/iris/handle/10665/128229.

1954

WHO Reg'l Office S.E. Asia, SEA/RC7/2, *Population Studies,* at 55 (1954) https://apps.who.int/iris/handle/10665/130998.

1955

World Population Conf., *Proceedings of the Conference,* U.N. Doc. E/CONF 13/412, (1955), https://documents-dds-ny.un.org/doc/UNDOC/GEN/NL5/502/64/PDF/NL550264.pdf?OpenElement.

1957

United Nations: G.A. Res. 1217 (XII) (Dec. 14, 1957), https://documents-dds-ny.un.org/doc/RESOLUTION/GEN/NR0/120/00/PDF/NR012000.pdf?OpenElement.

1962

WHO Executive Board, Res. EB29.R21, *On Communication from the International Fertility Association,* (Jan. 19, 1962), *in* 29th Sess. Geneva, 15-26 January 1962, Part I: Resolutions Annexes, (1962), https://apps.who.int/iris/handle/10665/87901.
World Health Organization [WHO], Res. WHA15.44,*On Communication from the International Fertility Association,* (May 24, 1962), *in* 15th World Health Assembly Geneva, 8-25 May 1962, Part I: Resolutions and Decisions, at 21 (1962), https://apps.who.int/iris/handle/10665/85748?locale-attribute=en&.
United Nations: G.A. Res. 1838 (XVII) (Dec. 18, 1962), https://digitallibrary.un.org/record/204294?ln=en.

1964

United Nations: Economic and Social Council Res. 1048 (XXXVII), A/18/P&B/4, Annex A (Apr. 27, 1965), https://apps.who.int/iris/handle/10665/136768?search-result=true&query=%22WHA18_PB-4%22&scope=%2F&rpp=10&sort_by=score&order=desc.

1965

WHO Executive Board Res. EB35.R31, *On Decisions of the United Nations affecting WHO's Activities: Resolution 1048 (XXXVII) of the Economic and Social Council,* (Jan. 27, 1965), 35th Sess. Geneva, 19-28 January 1965, Part I: Resolutions annexes, (1965), https://apps.who.int/iris/handle/10665/88958.
World Population Conf., *Proceedings of the Conference, Volume III: Projections measurement of Population Trends,* U.N. Doc. E/CONF.41/4, at B.8 pp. 267-308 (1965), https://documents-dds-ny.un.org/doc/UNDOC/GEN/N67/191/41/PDF/N6719141.pdf?OpenElement.
World Health Organization [WHO], *Programme Activities in the Health Aspects of World Population which might be Developed by WHO, Report by the Director-General,* 18th World Health Assembly, A18/P&B/4, pt. 1 annex 18, at 153-60 (Apr. 27, 1965), https://apps.who.int/iris/handle/10665/136768?search-result=true&query=A18%2FP%26B%2F4&scope=&rpp=10&sort_by=score&order=desc .
World Health Organization [WHO], Res. WHA18.49, *On Programme Activities in the Health Aspects of World Population Which might be Developed by WHO,* (May 21, 1965), 18th World Health Assembly Geneva, 4-21 May 1965, Part I: Resolutions and Decisions (1965) https://apps.who.int/iris/handle/10665/89329?search-result=true&query=WHA18.49&scope=&rpp=10&sort_by=score&order=desc.
United Nations: Economic and Social Council Res. 1084 (XXXIX), *On Work Programmes and Priorities in Population Fields,* (July 30, 1965), https://digitallibrary.un.org/record/214117?ln=en.

1966

World Health Organization [WHO], A19/P&B/19, *Programme Activities in the Health Aspects of World Population which might be Developed by WHO, Report by the Director-General,* (May 13, 1966), *in* 19th World Health Assembly Geneva, 3-20 May 1966, Part I: Resolutions and Decisions, annex 13 at 60-64 (1966), https://apps.who.int/iris/handle/10665/85788.
World Health Organization [WHO], Res. WHA19.43, *On Programme Activities in the Health Aspects of World Population which might be Developed by WHO,* (May 20, 1966), *in* 19th World Health Assembly Geneva, 3-20 May 1966, Part I: Resolutions and Decisions, (1966), https://apps.who.int/iris/handle/10665/89388?search-result=true&query=%22WHA19.43%22&scope=&rpp=10&sort_by=score&order=desc
United Nations: G.A. Res. 2211 (XXI), *On Population Growth and Economic Development,* (Sept. 7, 1966), https://undocs.org/Home/Mobile?FinalSymbol=a%2Fres%2F2211(XXI)&Language=E&DeviceType=Desktop&LangRequested=False.

1967

World Health Organization [WHO], A20/P&B/11,*Health Aspects of Population Dynamics: Report by the Director-General,* (May 4, 1967), *in* 20th World Health Assembly Geneva, 8-26 May 1967, Part I: Resolutions and Decisions, (1967) https://apps.who.int/iris/handle/10665/137602?search-result=true&query=A20%2FP%26B%2F11&scope=&rpp=10&sort_by=score&order=desc.
World Health Organization [WHO], Res. WHA20.41, *On Health Aspects of Population Dynamics,* (May 25, 1967), *in* 20th World Health Assembly Geneva, 8-26 May 1967 Part I: Resolutions and Decisions, (1967), https://apps.who.int/iris/handle/10665/89508?search-result=true&query=WHA20.41&scope=&rpp=10&sort_by=score&order=desc.

1968

World Health Organization [WHO], A21/P&B/9, *Health Aspects of Population Dynamics: Report by the Director-General*, (Apr. 24, 1968), *in* 21st World Health Assembly, Geneva, 6-24 May 1968, Part I: Resolutions and Decisions, (1968), https://apps.who.int/iris/handle/10665/143495?search-result=true&query=A21%2FP%26B%2F9&scope=%2F&rpp=10&sort_by=score&order=desc.
World Health Organization [WHO], Res. WHA21.43, *On Health Aspects of Population Dynamics*, (May 23, 1968), in 21st World Health Assembly Geneva, 6-24 May 1968, Part I: Resolutions and Decisions, (1968), https://apps.who.int/iris/handle/10665/91192?search-result=true&query=WHA21.43&scope=&rpp=10&sort_by=score&order=desc.

1969

World Health Organization [WHO], A22/P&B/11, *Health Aspects of Population Dynamics: Progress Report by the Director-General*, 22d World Health Assembly, Geneva, 8-25 July 1969, Part I: Resolutions and Decisions, (1969) https://apps.who.int/iris/handle/10665/144295?search-result=true&query=A22%2FP%26B%2F11&scope=&rpp=10&sort_by=score&order=desc.
World Health Organization [WHO], Res. WHA22.32, *On Health Aspects of Population Dynamics*, (July 23, 1969), *in* 22d World Health Assembly, Geneva, 8-25 July 1969, Part I: Resolutions and Decisions, at 13-14 (July 23, 1969), https://apps.who.int/iris/handle/10665/91257?search-result=true&query=WHA22.32&scope=&rpp=10&sort_by=score&order=desc.
WHO & Reg'l Comm. W. Pac., WRP/RC20/5, *Health Aspects of Population Dynamics: Report by the Regional Director*, (July 14, 1969), https://apps.who.int/iris/handle/10665/139174?search-result=true&query=Health+aspects+of+population+dynamics%3A+report+by+the+Director-General&scope=%2F&rpp=10&sort_by=score&order=desc.
WHO & Reg'l Comm. W. Pac, Res. WRP/RC20.R7, *On Health Aspects of Population Dynamics* (Sept. 29, 1969), https://apps.who.int/iris/handle/10665/358042?search-result=true&query=WPR%2FRC20.R7&scope=&rpp=10&sort_by=score&order=desc.
WHO & Reg'l Comm. Se. Asia, Res. SEA/RC22/R7, *On Health Aspects of Population Dynamics* (Oct. 3, 1969), https://apps.who.int/iris/handle/10665/130244?search-result=true&query=SEA%2FRC22%2FR7&scope=&rpp=10&sort_by=score&order=desc.

1971

World Health Organization [WHO], *The work of WHO 1970, Annual Report of the Director-General to the World Health Assembly and to the United Nations*, 74-76 (1971) https://apps.who.int/iris/handle/10665/85828.
World Health Organization [WHO], HR/71.4, *Expanded Programme of Research, Development and Research Training in Human Reproduction: Report of a Feasibility Project*; pt. 1 (1971), https://apps.who.int/iris/bitstream/handle/10665/361192/HR-71.4-Pt1-eng.pdf?sequence=1&isAllowed=y.
World Health Organization [WHO], HR/71.4, *Expanded Programme of Research, Development and Research Training in Human Reproduction Appendices: Report of a Feasibility Project*, pt. 2 (1971), https://apps.who.int/iris/bitstream/handle/10665/361192/HR-71.4-Pt2-eng.pdf?sequence=2&isAllowed=y.
World Health Organization [WHO], HR/71.4, *Expanded Programme of Research, Development and Research Training in Hunan Reproduction: Report of a Feasibility Project - Supplementary Information*, supp. 1 (1971), https://apps.who.int/iris/handle/10665/361193.
World Health Organization [WHO], *Proposed Programme and Budget Estimates for 1973*, pp. 100, 505, 610 (1971), https://apps.who.int/iris/handle/10665/85838.
World Health Organization [WHO], EB49/15, *Permanent Addition to the Headquarters Accommodation, Report by the Director-General*, (Nov. 26, 1971), https://apps.who.int/iris/handle/10665/145608?search-result=true&query=EB49%2F15&scope=&rpp=10&sort_by=score&order=desc.

1972

World Health Organization [WHO], *The Work of WHO 1971, Annual Report of the Director-General to the World Health Assembly and to the United Nations, 1972*, at 132-136 (1972) https://apps.who.int/iris/handle/10665/85845.
World Health Organization [WHO], *Report of the Director-General on the work of WHO in 1971*, 25th World Health Assembly Geneva, 9-26 May 1972, Part II: Plenary Meeting, Verbatim Records at 50-52 (1972), https://apps.who.int/iris/handle/10665/85851?search-result=true &query=Twenty-fifth+World+Health+Assembly%2C+Geneva%2C+9-26+may+1972&scope=&rpp=10&sort_by=score&order=desc.
World Health Organization [WHO], HR/71.9, *Expanded Programme of Research, Development and Research Training in Human Reproduction: Programme Strategy and Implementation,* (Jan. 6, 1972), https://apps.who.int/iris/handle/10665/361191.
A. Kessler, G. W. Perkin, & C.C. Standley, HR/71.9, 26 WHO Chronicle 46-55, (1972), https://apps.who.int/iris/handle/10665/361191.
WHO Executive Board Res. EB49.R33, *On Headquarters Accommodation: Future Requirements,*(Jan. 25, 1972), *in* 49th session, Geneva, 18-27 January 1972, part. I: Resolutions annexes, at 25 (1972), *https://apps.who.int/iris/handle/10665/85847?search-result=true&query=-+Executive+Board+–+Forty-Ninth+session%2C+Geneva%2C+18-27+January+1972&scope=%2F&rpp=10&sort_by=score&order=desc.*
WHO & Reg'l Comm. W.Pac., WPR/RC23/3, *Twenty-second Annual Report of the Regional Director to the Regional Committee for the Western Pacific Covering the Period, 1 July 1971 - 30 June 1972*, at 45 (1972), https://apps.who.int/iris/handle/10665/355243?search-result=true&query =WPR%2FRC23%2F3&scope=&rpp=10&sort_by=score&order=desc.
World Health Organization [WHO], *Expanded Programme of Research, Development and Research Training in Human Reproduction: Report on Programme Implementation during the First Year, October 1972*, HR/72.5a (1972), https://apps.who.int/iris/handle/10665/361194.
World Health Organization [WHO], Res. WHA25.60, *On WHO's Role in the Development and Coordination of Biomedical Research*, 25th World Health Assembly, Geneva, 9-26 May 1972 - Part I: resolutions and decisions, at 32-33 (1972), https://apps.who.int/iris/handle/10665/ 91995?search-result=true&query=WHA25.60&scope=&rpp= 10&sort_by=score&order=desc.
World Health Organization [WHO], EB51/6, *WHO's Role in the Development and Coordination of Biomedical Research: Interim Report by the Director-General,* (Dec. 1972), https://apps.who.int/iris/bitstream/ handle/10665/146302/EB51_6_eng.pdf?sequence=1&isAllowed=y.

1973

World Health Organization [WHO], *The work of WHO 1972, Annual Report of the Director-General to the World Health Assembly and to the United Nations,* 134-139 (1973), https://apps.who.int/iris/handle/10665/85854?search-result=true&query=The+work+of+WHO+1972%2C&scope=&rpp=10&sort_by=score&order=desc
World Health Organization [WHO], Address by the President of the Assembly, *in* 26th World Health Assembly, Geneva, 7-23 May 1973: part II: verbatim records of plenary meetings, 60-61 (1973), https://apps.who.int/iris/handle/10665/85863.
World Health Organization [WHO], HR/73.5a, *Expanded Programme of Research, Development and Research Training in Human Reproduction: Second annual report, November 1973,* (1973), https://apps.who.int/iris/handle/10665/361196.
World Health Organization [WHO], HR/73.5c, *Expanded Programme of Research, Development and Research Training in Human Reproduction: projections 1974-1976, November 1973,* (1973), https://apps.who.int/iris/handle/10665/361197.
World Health Organization [WHO], Res. WHA26.42, *On WHO's Role in the Development and Coordination of Biomedical Research,* 26th World Health Assembly, Geneva, 7-23 May 1973: part I: resolutions and decisions, at 24 (1973), https://apps.who.int/iris/handle/10665/92135?search-result=true&query=WHA26.42&scope=&rpp=10&sort_by=score&order=desc.
World Health Organization [WHO], EB53/5, *WHO's Role in the Development and Coordination of Biomedical Research: Report by the Director-General,* at 3 §B.3 (Dec. 1973), https://apps.who.int/iris/handle/10665/147104.

1974

WHO, EB55/8, *WHO's Role in the Development and Coordination of Biomedical Research: Progress Report by the Director-General,* (Dec. 1974), https://apps.who.int/iris/bitstream/handle/10665/148377/EB55_8_eng.pdf?sequence=1&isAllowed=y.
WHO Res. WHA27.61, *On WHO's Role in the Development and Coordination of Biomedical Research,* 27th World Health Assembly, Geneva, 7-23 May 1974: part I: resolutions and decisions, at 31 (1974), https://apps.who.int/iris/handle/10665/92782?search-result=true&query=WHA27.61&scope=&rpp=10&sort_by=score&order=desc.
World Health Organization [WHO], Res. WHA27.30, *On World Population Year and Conference, 1974,* (May 21, 1974), *in* 27th World Health Assembly Geneva Part. I: Resolutions and Decisions, at 13-14 (1974), https://apps.who.int/iris/handle/10665/85874.
World Health Organization [WHO], EB55/43, *World Population Year and Conference 1974, Report by the Director-General,* (Dec. 5, 1974) https://apps.who.int/iris/handle/10665/148831?search-result=true&query=EB55%2F43&scope=&rpp=10&sort_by=score&order=desc.

1975

World Health Organization [WHO], Res. WHA28.44, *On World Population Year and Conference, 1974,* (May 28, 1975), *in* 28th World Health Assembly Geneva, 13-30 May 1975, Part I Resolutions and Decisions, at 22-23 (1975), https://apps.who.int/iris/handle/10665/92942?search-result=true&query=%22WHA28.44%22&scope=%2F&rpp=10&sort_by=score&order=desc.
WHO Executive Board Res. EB55.R60, *On Coordination with Other Organizations of the United Nations System: World Population Year and Conference, 1974,* (January 31, 1975), *in* 56th session, Geneva, 20-31 January 1975, Part I: resolutions: annexes (1975), https://apps.who.int/iris/bitstream/handle/10665/90743/EB55R60_eng.pdf?sequence=1&isAllowed=y

1977

World Health Organization [WHO], A30/9, *Development and Coordination of Biomedical and Health Services Research: Report by the Director-General,* (1977), https://apps.who.int/iris/handle/10665/149098?search-result=true&query=A30%2F9&scope=&rpp=10&sort_by=score&order=desc.
World Health Organization [WHO], EB61/23, *Development and Coordination of Biomedical and Health Services Research: Report by the Director-General,* (Dec. 1, 1977), *in* Special Programme of Research, Development and Research Training in Human Reproduction, Annex I at 7-15 (1977), https://apps.who.int/iris/handle/10665/153639?search-result=true&query=EB61%2F23&scope=&rpp=10&sort_by=score&order=desc.
World Health Organization [WHO], Res. WHA30.40, *On Development and Coordination of Biomedical and Health Services Research,* (May 18, 1977), *in* 30th World Health Assembly, Geneva, 2-19 May 1977 - Part I Resolutions and Decisions, at 22-23 (1977), https://apps.who.int/iris/handle/10665/93203?search-result=true&query=WHA30.40&scope=&rpp=10&sort_by=score&order=desc.

1978

World Health Organization [WHO], A31/16, *Special Programme of Research, Development and Research Training in Human Reproduction, Report by the Director-General,* (1978), https://apps.who.int/iris/handle/10665/149774?search-result=true&query=%22A31%2F16%22&scope=%2F&rpp=10&sort_by=score&order=desc
World Health Organization [WHO] Res. WHA31.37, *On Special Programme of Research, Development and Research Training in Human Reproduction,* (May 23, 1978), *in* 31st World Health Assembly Geneva, 8-24 May 1978, Part I Resolutions and Decisions, at 24-25 (1978), https://apps.who.int/iris/handle/10665/93435.
World Health Organization [WHO], EB63/PC/WP/7, *Programme Committee of the Executive Board: Development and Coordination of Biomedical and Health Services Research: Progress Report by the Director-General,* (1978), https://apps.who.int/iris/handle/10665/154059?search-result=true&query=EB63%2FPC%2FWP%2F7&scope=&rpp=10&sort_by=score&order=desc.

1979

World Health Organization [WHO], EB65/20, *Development and Coordination of Biomedical and Health Services Research: Report by the Director-General*, (1979), https://apps.who.int/iris/handle/10665/154398?search-result=true&query=EB65%2F20&scope=&rpp=10&sort_by=score&order=desc.
World Health Organization [WHO], Res. WHA32.15, *On Development and Coordination of Biomedical and Health Services Research*, (May 22, 1979), *in* 32d World Health Assembly, Geneva, 7-25 May 1979: resolutions and decisions, at 14-15 (1979), https://apps.who.int/iris/handle/10665/154319?search-result=true&query=WHA32.15&scope=&rpp=10&sort_by=score&order=desc.
World Health Organization [WHO], Res. WHA32.30, *On Formulating Strategies for Health for All by the Year 2000*, (May 22, 1979), *in* 32d World Health Assembly, Geneva, 7-25 May 1979: resolutions and decisions, at 27-29 (1979), https://apps.who.int/iris/handle/10665/154334?search-result=true&query=WHA32.30&scope=&rpp=10&sort_by=score&order=desc.

1980

World Health Organization [WHO], A33/9, *Development and Coordination of Biomedical and Health Services Research: Progress Report by the Director-General*, (Apr. 3, 1980), https://apps.who.int/iris/handle/10665/154539?search-result=true&query=%22A33%2F9%22&scope=%2F&rpp=10&sort_by=score&order=desc.
World Health Organization [WHO], Res. WHA33.25, *On Development and Coordination of Biomedical and Health Services Research*, (May 23, 1980), *in* 33d World Health Assembly, Geneva, 5-23 May 1980, resolutions and decisions, at 25-26 (1980), https://apps.who.int/iris/handle/10665/155550?search-result=true&query=WHA33.25&scope=&rpp=10&sort_by=score&order=desc.

1981

World Health Organization [WHO], A34/3, *Report of the Director-General on the work of WHO in 1980*, (Apr. 1, 1981), *in* 34th World Health Assembly Geneva, 4-22 May 1981, Resolutions and Decisions, Annex 4 §§ 56, 101-105, 109 (1981), https://apps.who.int/iris/handle/10665/155588?search-result=true&query=A34%2F3&scope=&rpp=10&sort_by=score&order=desc.

U.N. Economic and Social Council Res. E/RES/1981/28, *On Strengthening of Actions Concerned with the Fulfilment of the World Population Plan of Action*, §4 (May 6, 1981), https://digitallibrary.un.org/record/32816?ln=fr#record-files-collapse-header.

1982

World Health Organization [WHO], A35/17, *Collaboration with the United Nations system: general matters: report by the Director-General*, at 10 § 5.14 (Apr. 2, 1982), https://apps.who.int/iris/bitstream/handle/10665/156743/WHA35_17_eng.pdf?sequence=1&isAllowed=y

1983

World Health Organization [WHO], A36/3, *Report of the Director-General on the work of WHO in 1982*, (March 24, 1983), *in* 36th World Health Assembly Geneva, 2-16 May 1983, Resolutions and Decisions, Annex 8 § 103 (1983), https://apps.who.int/iris/handle/10665/159408?search-result=true&query=A36%2F3&scope=&rpp=10&sort_by=score&order=desc.

WHO & S.E. Asia Advisory Comm. on Med. Rsch., SEA/ACMR/9/11, *Special Programme on Research Development and Research Training in Human Reproduction*, (Feb. 21, 1983), https://apps.who.int/iris/handle/10665/127360.

1987

World Health Organization [WHO], A40/3, *Report of the Director-General on the work of WHO in 1986,* (February 18, 1987), *in* 40th World Health Assembly, Geneva, 4-15 May 1987, Resolutions and Decisions, Annex 6 at 90, 98 (1987), https://apps.who.int/iris/handle/10665/163838.
World Health Organization [WHO], EB81/22, *Recent Developments in Human Reproduction Research, Progress Report by the Director-General,* (1987), https://apps.who.int/iris/handle/10665/162389.
W.Pac. Reg'l Comm., *Special Program for Research, Development and Training in Human Reproduction: Composition of the Advisory Committee on Guiding Principles and Coordination (resolution), WHO Regional Office for the Western Pacific,* (1987), https://apps.who.int/iris/handle/10665/360765.

1988

WHO Executive Board Res. EB81.R6, *On Special Programme of Research, Development and Research Training in Human Reproduction,* (January 15, 1988), *in* 81st session, Geneva, 11-20 January 1988, Resolutions and Decisions, at 3-4 (1988), https://apps.who.int/iris/handle/10665/162488?search-result=true&query=EB81.R6&scope=&rpp=10&sort_by=score&order=desc.
World Health Organization [WHO], WHA41/1988/REC/3, *Special Programme of Research, Development and Research Training in Human Reproduction,* (May 9, 1988), *in* 41st World Health Assembly, Geneva, 2-13 May 1988, at 35-43 (1988), https://apps.who.int/iris/handle/10665/164199?search-result=true&query=WHA41%2F1988%2FREC%2F3&scope=&rpp=10&sort_by=score&order=desc.
World Health Organization [WHO], Res. WHA41.9, *On Special Programme of Research, Development and Research Training in Human Reproduction,* (May 11, 1988), *in* 41st World Health Assembly, Geneva, 2-13 May 1988, Resolutions and Decisions, at 6-7 (1988), https://apps.who.int/iris/handle/10665/164346?search-result=true&query=WHA41.9&scope=&rpp=10&sort_by=score&order=desc.
World Health Organization [WHO], HRP/1988/1, *Memorandum on the Administrative Structure of the Special Programme of Research, Development and Research Training in Human Reproduction,* (1988), https://www.who.int/docs/default-source/hrp/hrp-admin-structure.pdf?sfvrsn=c01d0a2d_2.
World Health Organization [WHO], *Research in Human Reproduction, Biennial Report 1986-1987,* (1988), https://apps.who.int/iris/handle/10665/42106.

1989

World Health Organization [WHO], A42/3, *Report of the Director-General on the work of WHO in 1988, in* 42d World Health Assembly, Geneva, 8-13 May 1989, Part I: Resolutions and Decisions, Annex 7 at 168-69 (1989), https://apps.who.int/iris/handle/10665/171211?locale-attribute=fr&.
World Health Organization [WHO], A42/10, *Expanded Programme on Immunization, Progress and Evaluation Report, in* 42d World Health Assembly, Geneva, 8-13 May 1989, Part I: Resolutions and Decisions, annex 6 at 135 (1989), https://apps.who.int/iris/handle/10665/171211?locale-attribute=fr&.
World Health Organization [WHO], A/42/9, *WHO's Contribution to the International Efforts towards Sustainable Development, Report of the Director-General, in* 42d World Health Assembly, Geneva, 8-13 May 1989, Part I: Resolutions and Decisions, annex 4 at 89, 93 (1989), https://apps.who.int/iris/handle/10665/171211?locale-attribute=fr&.

1990

World Health Organization [WHO], *Research in Human Reproduction, Biennial Report 1988-1989,* (1990), https://apps.who.int/iris/handle/10665/38601.

1992

World Health Organization [WHO], *Reproductive Health: a Key to a Brighter Future, Biennial Report 1990-1991, Special 20th Anniversary issue,* (1992), https://apps.who.int/iris/handle/10665/38595.

1993

World Health Organization [WHO], A46/3, *Report of the Director-General on the work of WHO,* (Apr. 7, 1993), *in* 46th World Health Assembly, Geneva, 3-14 May 1993, Resolutions and Decisions, annex 13 at 168-69 (1993), https://apps.who.int/iris/handle/10665/176262?locale-attribute=ru&.
World Health Organization [WHO], WHO/MCH/FPP/92.3, *Natural Family Planning Methods: What Health Workers Need to Know,* § 70 (1993), https://apps.who.int/iris/handle/10665/65252.

1994

WHO, *Challenges in Reproductive Health Research: Biennial Report: 1992-1993*, at 9-20 (1994), https://apps.who.int/iris/handle/10665/39653.

1995

World Health Organization [WHO], A48/10, *Maternal and Child Health and Family Planning: Quality of Care Reproductive Health: WHO's Role in the Global Strategy, Report by the Director-General,* (Apr. 24, 1995), 48th World Health Assembly, Geneva, 1-12 May 1995, Resolutions and Decisions, annex 2 at 54-65 (1995), https://apps.who.int/iris/handle/10665/177489?search-result=true&query=A48%2F10&scope=&rpp=10&sort_by=score&order=desc.
World Health Organization [WHO], Res. WHA48.10, *On Reproductive Health: WHO's Role in the Global Strategy,* (May 12, 1995), *in* 48th World Health Assembly, Geneva, 1-12 May 1995, Resolutions and Decisions, at 11-12 (1995), https://apps.who.int/iris/handle/10665/178406.

1998

World Health Organization [WHO], *Reproductive Health Research, the New Directions, Biennial Report: 1996-1997,* (1998), https://apps.who.int/iris/handle/10665/42105?locale-attribute=pt&.
World Health Organization [WHO], *Division of Reproductive Health (Technical Support): Progress Report,* (1998), https://apps.who.int/iris/handle/10665/70123.

1999

World Health Organization [WHO], *Division of Reproductive Health (Technical Support): Progress report 1998,* (1999), https://apps.who.int/iris/handle/10665/70123.
World Health Organization [WHO], *Division of Reproductive Health (Technical Support): Progress report 1998,* (1999), https://apps.who.int/iris/handle/10665/70123.

2000

World Health Organization [WHO], *Reproductive Health Research in WHO: a New Beginning HRP Financial Report 1998-1999* (2000), https://apps.who.int/iris/handle/10665/66327.

2001

World Health Organization: *HRP annual technical report,* (2001), https://apps.who.int/iris/handle/10665/59249.
World Health Organization [WHO], *Unaudited Interim Financial Report for the Year 2000: Fiscal 2000-2001,* 54th World Health Assembly (2001), https://apps.who.int/iris/handle/10665/83758
World Health Organization [WHO], *Research on Reproductive Health at WHO, Biennial Report: 2000-2001* (2002), https://apps.who.int/iris/bitstream/handle/10665/42505/9241562080_eng.pdf?sequence=1&isAllowed=y.

2002

World Health Organization [WHO], *Research on Reproductive Health at WHO, Biennial Report: 2000-2001,* (2002), https://apps.who.int/iris/bitstream/handle/10665/42505/9241562080_eng.pdf?sequence=1&isAllowed=y.
World Health Organization [WHO], *HRP Annual Technical Report,* (2002), https://apps.who.int/iris/handle/10665/42726.
World Health Organization [WHO], *Report on the in-depth Review of Research Capacity Strengthening by HRP/WHO,* (2002), https://apps.who.int/iris/handle/10665/67298.
World Health Organization [WHO], Res. WHA55.19, *On WHO's Contribution to Achievement of the Development Goals of the United Nations Millennium Declaration,* (May 18, 2002), https://apps.who.int/iris/handle/10665/78536?search-result=true&query=WHA55.19&scope=&rpp=10&sort_by=score&order=desc.

2003

World Health Organization [WHO], *HRP, Highlights of Achievements 1990-2001,* (2003), https://apps.who.int/iris/handle/10665/67805.
World Health Organization [WHO], *External Evaluation 1990-2002: Executive Summary,* (2003), https://apps.who.int/iris/handle/10665/68509.

2004

World Health Organization [WHO], *Research on Reproductive Health at WHO: Pushing the Frontiers of Knowledge: Biennial Report 2002-2003*, (2004), https://apps.who.int/iris/handle/10665/42997.
World Health Organization [WHO], *Follow-up Measures to the External Evaluation of HRP for the Period 1990-2002*, (2004), https://apps.who.int/iris/handle/10665/68625.
World Health Organization [WHO], *External Evaluation 1990-2002: Executive Summary*, (2004), https://apps.who.int/iris/handle/10665/68640.
World Health Organization [WHO], Res. WHA57.12, *On Reproductive Health: Draft Strategy to Accelerate Progress towards the Attainment of International Development Goals and Targets*, (May 22, 2004), https://apps.who.int/iris/bitstream/handle/10665/20137/A57_R12-en.pdf?sequence=1&isAllowed=y.
World Health Organization [WHO], *Reproductive Health Strategy to Accelerate Progress Towards the Attainment of International Development Goals and Targets*, (2004), https://apps.who.int/iris/handle/10665/68754.

2006

World Health Organization [WHO], *Sexual and Reproductive Health: Laying the Foundation for a more just World through Research and Action, Biennial Report 2004-2005*, at 14 (2006), https://apps.who.int/iris/handle/10665/43497.

2008

World Health Organization [WHO], *Sexual and Reproductive Health: Research and Action in Support of the Millennium Development Goals, Biennial Report 2006-2007,* (2008), https://apps.who.int/iris/handle/10665/43916.
World Health Organization [WHO], *Providing the foundation for sexual and reproductive health: a record of achievement,* (2008), https://apps.who.int/iris/handle/10665/70757.
World Health Organization [WHO], *External Evaluation 2003-2007: Monitoring Governance, Management, Administration and Efficiency: a Case Study,* (2008), https://apps.who.int/iris/handle/10665/69895.
World Health Organization [WHO], *External Evaluation 2003-2007: Improving the Safety and Effectiveness of Contraception in China: a Case-study in Promotion and Improvement of Family Planning,* (2008), https://apps.who.int/iris/handle/10665/69909.
World Health Organization [WHO], *External Evaluation 2003-2007: Long-term Safety and Effectiveness of Copper-releasing Intrauterine Devices: Case Study,* (2008), https://apps.who.int/iris/handle/10665/69908.
World Health Organization [WHO], *External Evaluation 2003-2007: Knowledge Synthesis and Transfer: a Case Study,* (2008), https://apps.who.int/iris/handle/10665/69905.
World Health Organization [WHO], *External Evaluation 2003-2007: Impact of HRP Research in Medical (Non-surgical) Induced Abortion: a Case Study,* (2008), https://apps.who.int/iris/handle/10665/69907.
World Health Organization [WHO], *External Evaluation 2003-2007: Impact of HRP Research in Maternal and Perinatal Care: a Case Study,* (2008), https://apps.who.int/iris/handle/10665/69906.
World Health Organization [WHO], *External Evaluation 2003-2007: Executive Summary,* (2008), https://apps.who.int/iris/handle/10665/69889.

2009

World Health Organization [WHO], *HRP Highlights of 2008*, (2009), https://apps.who.int/iris/handle/10665/70062.
World Health Organization [WHO], *Teaching the Basics of Sexual and Reproductive Health: a Review of Achievements*, (2009), https://apps.who.int/iris/handle/10665/70767.
World Health Organization [WHO], *Review of Global Work of WHO on Health Research: HRP*, (2009), https://apps.who.int/iris/handle/10665/127184.

2010

World Health Organization [WHO], *Biennial report of HRP 2008-2009*, (2010), https://apps.who.int/iris/handle/10665/70346.
World Health Organization [WHO], *HRP Highlights 2009*, (2010), https://apps.who.int/iris/handle/10665/70347.
World Health Organization [WHO], *RHR Highlights 2009*, (2010), https://apps.who.int/iris/handle/10665/70348.

2011

World Health Organization [WHO], *HRP Highlights of 2010*, (2011), https://apps.who.int/iris/handle/10665/70726.
World Health Organization [WHO], *Highlights of 2010*, (2011), https://apps.who.int/iris/handle/10665/70722.
World Health Organization [WHO], *HRP Biennial Technical Report 2009-2010*, (2011), https://apps.who.int/iris/handle/10665/44617.
World Health Organization [WHO], *WHO Sexual and Reproductive Health Medium-term Strategic Plan for 2010-2015 and Programme Budget for 2012-2013* (2011), https://apps.who.int/iris/handle/10665/78068.

2012

World Health Organization [WHO], *Highlights of 2011*, (2012), https://apps.who.int/iris/handle/10665/70928.
World Health Organization [WHO], *HRP at 40: What They Say: a History of Scientific Achievement to Advance Sexual and Reproductive Health*, (2012), https://apps.who.int/iris/handle/10665/70911.
World Health Organization [WHO], *Memorandum on the Administrative Structure of the Special Programme of Research, Development and Research Training in Human Reproduction (HRP)*, (2012), https://cdn.who.int/media/docs/default-source/hrp/hrp-mou-admin-structure-rev-2012.pdf?sfvrsn=de99f821_2.

2013

World Health Organization [WHO], *HRP Highlights of 2012*, (2013), https://apps.who.int/iris/handle/10665/85154.
World Health Organization [WHO], *Annual Technical Report: HRP 2012*, (2013), https://apps.who.int/iris/handle/10665/84992.
World Health Organization [WHO], *External Evaluation 2008-2012: Advancing Sexual and Reproductive Health*, (2013), https://apps.who.int/iris/handle/10665/85331.
World Health Organization [WHO], *External Evaluation 2008-2012: Advancing Sexual and Reproductive Health: Executive Summary*, (2013), https://apps.who.int/iris/handle/10665/85332.

2014

World Health Organization [WHO], *HRP Highlights of 2013*, (2014), https://apps.who.int/iris/handle/10665/112763.
World Health Organization [WHO], *Annual Technical Report: HRP 2013*, (2014), https://apps.who.int/iris/handle/10665/112658.

2015

World Health Organization [WHO], *HRP Highlights of 2014*, (2015), https://apps.who.int/iris/handle/10665/153841.
World Health Organization [WHO], *Annual Technical Report: HRP 2014*, (2015), https://apps.who.int/iris/handle/10665/171613.

2016

World Health Organization [WHO], *HRP Highlights of 2015*, (2016), https://apps.who.int/iris/handle/10665/206544.
World Health Organization [WHO], *Annual Technical Report 2015*, (2016), https://apps.who.int/iris/handle/10665/246092.

2017

World Health Organization [WHO], *HRP Annual Report 2016*, (2017), https://apps.who.int/iris/handle/10665/255768.

2018

World Health Organization [WHO], *HRP Annual Report 2017*, (2018), https://apps.who.int/iris/handle/10665/260493.

2019

World Health Organization [WHO], *HRP Annual Report 2018*, (2019), https://apps.who.int/iris/handle/10665/310956.
World Health Organization [WHO], *External Evaluation of the UNDP-UNFPA-UNICEF-WHO-World Bank Special Programme of Research, Development and Research Training in Human Reproduction (HRP) 2013-2017*, (2019), https://cdn.who.int/media/docs/default-source/hrp/hrp-evaluation-report-vol-1.pdf?sfvrsn=140faddc_6&download=true.

2020

World Health Organization [WHO], *HRP Annual Report 2019*, (2020), https://apps.who.int/iris/handle/10665/331637.

2021

World Health Organization [WHO], *HRP Annual Report 2020* (2021), https://apps.who.int/iris/handle/10665/346657.

2022

World Health Organization [WHO], *Reflections on a Dream Job in Sexual and Reproductive Health and Rights*, (February 2022) https://www.who.int/news/item/20-02-2022-reflections-on-a-dream-job-in-sexual-and-reproductive-health-and-rights

Appendix 4 – Bibliography

Albert Zahra & Richard Strudwick, *The Role of the World Health Organization in Health Related Aspects of Family Planning*, 3 INT'L J. HEALTH SERVS. 701-07 (1973), http://www.jstor.org/stable/45132156.

Alexander Kessler & Constance C. Standley, *Human Reproduction and Family Planning: Research Strategies in Developing Countries*, 251 NATURE 577-79 (1974).

Jason L. Finkle & Barbara B. Crane, *The World Health Organization and the Population Issue: Organizational Values in the United Nations*, 2 POPULATION AND DEV. REV. 367-93 (1976), https://doi.org/10.2307/1971616 https://cutt.ly/4HY7XG8.

Alexander Kessler & Constance C. Standley, *The WHO Expanded Programme of Research, Development and Research Training in Human Reproduction*, ROYAL SOC'Y BIOLOGICAL SCI. 129-36 (1976).

Alexander Kessler & Constance C. Standley, *Research on Birth Control Technology*, INTERDISC. SCI. REVS. 196-201 (1978), http://dx.doi.org/10.1179/030801878791926038.

Egon Diczfalusy, *World Health Organization Special Programme of Research, Development and Research Training in Human Reproduction. An International Response to a Global Concern*, 32 CONTRACEPTION 323-36 (Oct. 1985).

Egon Diczfalusy, *The First Fifteen Years*, 34 CONTRACEPTION 1-119 (1986).

Rouzé Michel, *Plus fort que la pilule : le vaccin contraceptif* [*Stronger than the Pill: the contraceptive vaccine*], RAISON PRÉSENTE, at 143 (1986), https://www.persee.fr/doc/raipr_0033-9075_1986_num_79_1_2536_t1_0143_0000_2.

Ron Lesthaege, *On the Social Control of Human Reproduction*, 6 POPULATION & DEV. REV. 527-48 (1990), http://www.jstor.org/stable/1972925.

W. Parker Mauldin & John A. Ross, *Family Planning Programs: Efforts and Results*, 22 STUD. FAM. PLAN. 350-67 (1991).

Giuseppe 65/20 & Egon Diczfalusy, *Research on Human Reproduction and the United Nations*, 85 S. AFR. MED. J. 370, 371-73 (1995).

Nelly Oudshoorn, *From Population Control Politics to Chemicals: The WHO as an Intermediary Organization in Contraceptive Development*, 27 SOC. STUD. SCIENCE 41-72 (1997), https://doi.org/10.1177/030631297027001003.

Choquette Catherine & Obijiofor Aginam, *Global Health Governance: International Law and Public Health in a Divided World* (2005), *reprinted in* 20-1 QUEBEC J. L. INT'L 461-62 (2007).

Yves Beigbeder, *World Health Organization Partnerships*, 41 INT'L STUD. 233-51 (2010), https://doi.org/10.7202/044615ar.

World Health Organization, *World Health Statistics 2010*, (WHO Library, 2010), https://books.google.fr/books?hl=fr&lr=&id=Z69vxfRfFIsC&oi=fnd&pg=PA1&dq=world+health+organization+demographic+data&ots=cINMbkJH8B&sig=gYKssxbAN1trE23s6ehbkgPrAyA#v=onepage&q=world%20health%20organization%20demographic%20data&f=true.

Paul Demeny, *Population Policy and the Demographic Transition: Performance, Prospects, and Options*, 37 POPULATION & DEV. REV. 249-74 (2011), https://doi.org/10.1111/j.1728-4457.2011.00386.x.

Michael T Mbizvo, Catherine d'Arcangues, Paul FA Van Look, & Benagiano Giuseppe, *40 Years of Innovation in Sexual and Reproductive Health*, 380 THE LANCET 705-06 (2012).

Giuseppe Benagiano et al., *The Special Programme of Research in Human Reproduction: Forty Years of Activities to Achieve Reproductive Health for All*, 74 GYNECOLOGIC & OBSTETRIC INVESTIGATION 190-217 (2012).

Erika Dyck, *Reproductive rights*, THE EUGENIC ARCHIVE (2014), https://eugenicsarchive.ca/discover/encyclopedia/535eedec7095aa0000000253, (viewed May 18, 2022).

Virginie De Luca Barrusse &Anne-Françoise Praz, *Population Policies: Resituating the Object of research*, 129 ANNALS OF HIST. DEMOGRAPHY 149-64 (2015), https://doi.org/10.3917/adh.129.0149.

John F. May, *Population Policies in Europe*, 377 EUROPE IN FORMATION 136-50 (2015), https://doi.org/10.3917/eufor.377.0136.

Tiloka de Silva & Silvana Tenreyro, *Population Control Policies and Fertility Convergence*, 31 J. ECON. PERSPS. 205-28 (2017).

Paul Lombardo, *Eugenics and Public Health: Historical Connections and Ethical Implications, in*, THE OXFORD HANDBOOK OF PUBLIC HEALTH ETHICS, 642-52

(Anna C. Mastroianni, Jeffrey P. Kahn, & Nancy E. Kass eds., 2019), https://doi.org/10.1093/oxfordhb/9780190245191.013.56.

Rebecca Sear, *Demography and the Rise, Apparent Fall, and Resurgence of Eugenics*, 75 POPULATION STUD. 201-20 (2021), https://doi.org/10.1080/00324728.2021.2009013.

William J. Ripple et al., *World Scientists' Warning of a Climate Emergency 2021*, 71 BIOSCIENCE 894-98 (2021), https://doi.org/10.1093/biosci/biab079.

Eneyi E. Kpokiri et al., *Development of an International Sexual and Reproductive Health Survey Instrument: Results from a Pilot WHO/HRP Consultative Delphi Process*, 98 SEXUALLY TRANSMITTED INFECTIONS 38-43 (Feb. 2022).

Index

www.ingramcontent.com/pod-product-compliance
Ingram Content Group UK Ltd.
Pitfield, Milton Keynes, MK11 3LW, UK
UKHW041133071026
15587UKWH00009B/476

9 781804 413838